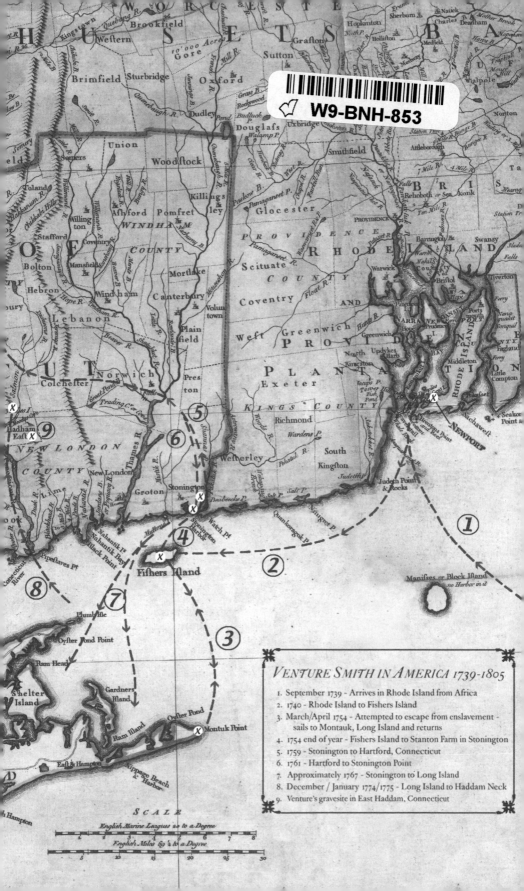

W9-BNH-853

VENTURE SMITH IN AMERICA 1739-1805

1. September 1739 - Arrives in Rhode Island from Africa
2. 1740 - Rhode Island to Fishers Island
3. March/April 1754 - Attempted to escape from enslavement - sails to Montauk, Long Island and returns
4. 1754 end of year - Fishers Island to Stanton Farm in Stonington
5. 1759 - Stonington to Hartford, Connecticut
6. 1761 - Hartford to Stonington Point
7. Approximately 1767 - Stonington to Long Island
8. December / January 1774/1775 - Long Island to Haddam Neck
9. Venture's gravesite in East Haddam, Connecticut

SCALE

English Marine Leagues 20 to a Degree

English Miles 69 ½ to a Degree

MAKING FREEDOM

MAKING FREEDOM

THE EXTRAORDINARY LIFE OF VENTURE SMITH

Chandler B. Saint

&

George A. Krimsky

WESLEYAN UNIVERSITY PRESS
Middletown, Connecticut

Published by

Wesleyan University Press,

Middletown, CT 06459

www.wesleyan.edu/wespress

Saint, Chandler B.

Making freedom : the extraordinary life of Venture Smith / Chandler B.

Saint and George A. Krimsky.

p. cm.   Includes bibliographical references and index.

ISBN 978-0-8195-6854-0 (cloth : alk. paper)

1. Smith, Venture, 1729?-1805. 2. Slaves--Connecticut--Biography.

3. Free African Americans--Connecticut--Biography. 4. African

Americans--Connecticut--Biography. 5. Slavery--Connecticut--History--18th

century. 6. Connecticut--Race relations--History--18th century. 7. Haddam

(Conn.)--Biography. I. Krimsky, George A. II. Title.

E444.S625S25 2008   306.3'62092--dc22

[B]

2008029052

9 8 7 6 5 4 3 2 1

To

Rachel Freeman Saint

(1906–2007)

CONTENTS

❖┄◄┄◄┄◄◉◈◉►┄►┄►┄❖

"It's important his story be told and spread throughout all the United States, because it's such a positive African-American story."

– DAVID P. WARMSLEY, eighth-generation descendant of Venture Smith

FOREWORD

The story of Venture Smith is an important part of American history. In many ways, it is an American story of the struggle for freedom. Yet Venture struggled against a powerful American institution, the institution of slavery. The capture and enslavement of this one African in 18th-century America before the North American British colonies began their own freedom struggle, which led ultimately to national independence, illustrate the young nation's most fundamental contradiction. American patriots explained their revolution against the British monarchy as a natural result of their dedication to human rights and human liberty. However, by holding tens of thousands of Africans as slaves, the new United States of America diminished much of its moral authority in the eyes of the world. In its Declaration of Independence, written by Thomas Jefferson, a Virginia slaveholder with one hundred and fifty bound people in his possession when he penned the words, the nation asserted its commitment to the basic, God-given human rights of "life, liberty and the pursuit of happiness."

The irony of slaveholders publicly declaring their commitment to human freedom did not go unnoticed at home or abroad. As founding father John Adams worked to establish American liberty, his wife Abigail pointed forcefully to the contradiction. In a letter to her husband in 1774 she reflected on the state of freedom in America. "It always appeard a most iniquitous scheme to me," she wrote, "to fight ourselves for what we are daily robbing and plundering from those who have as good a right to freedom as we have."[1]

British writer Samuel Johnson directly challenged the American argument for its independence. In his 1775 pamphlet, *Taxation No Tyranny*, Johnson defended the right of the king to rule over his American subjects, and then posed a stinging question: "How is it that we hear the loudest yelps for liberty among the drivers of [N]egroes?"[2]

Venture and the other African slaves held in this emerging free nation could not have agreed more. In 1773 and 1774 Massachusetts slaves confronted colonial authorities with the question of their freedom. "We expect great things from men who have made such a noble stand against the designs of their fellow men to enslave them," they declared. The slaves demanded that they be allowed one day a week to labor for their own benefit so they might accumulate funds to purchase their own freedom. This petition was refused, but others followed, each carefully worded to highlight the parallels between their cause and the colonists' desire for a "free and Christian country."[3] Yet, as America struggled for its national independence, slavery remained a vital institution, surely in the southern and middle Atlantic regions of the young nation, but even in much of New England. In Vermont, where slaveholdings were never large, slavery was abolished altogether in its constitution of 1777. In Massachusetts, with a much larger and more economically significant slave presence, in 1783 the supreme court of the commonwealth ruled slavery illegal under the constitution of 1780. Still, in Connecticut, where Venture Smith spent more than half his life, slavery was a powerful institution in the 18th century. By 1774, New London County had become the greatest slave-holding section of New England, with almost twice as many slaves as the most populous slave county in Massachusetts. As the Revolution approached, Connecticut had more than 6,000 slaves, the largest number of any colony in New England.[4]

Venture was sold from master to master until 1760, when he was able to strike a deal that allowed him to buy his freedom on a time payment plan. Five years later he had worked his way out of slavery, taking on a variety of jobs and seizing what little opportunity was available to black people in revolutionary America. On the eve of the Revolution that would bring liberty to white Americans, Venture Smith was able to purchase the freedom of his wife and three children, bringing his entire family out of bondage. As the American colonies waged their freedom struggle against British power, Venture purchased a farm in the small Connecticut village of Haddam, on the Connecticut River. There he would live the rest of his life as a prominent landowner and businessman.

As the nation matured through its revolutionary years, slavery was gradually ended in most of the northern states. Venture and his family settled into a more secure freedom in New England, but in the South, slaveholders gained increased economic and political power. During the first quarter of the 19th century, as the cotton curtain descended on the South, expanding into the rich black-belt regions of the Louisiana territory, a slave's achievement of freedom for himself and his family there became all but impossible. Thus, Venture Smith's accomplishment was attributable in part to opportunities available to the enslaved at a specific time and place. Antislavery voices in New England benefited from the fact that slavery was never as strong there as it was, and would continue to be, in the South. The call to reconcile America's commitment to freedom with its tolerance of slave labor was strong in revolutionary-era New England.

In the South, however, slavery remained a stubbornly solid institution from which there was but small chance of escape. Venture Smith's story then is an important reminder of the power of slavery and race in the formation of the American story in all parts of the nation and of the regional separation on the issue that led to America's most costly war. It also remains an uncomfortable story for those who would rather not face the hypocrisy of this part of the nation's history.

Venture Smith's story is also the iconic story of a self-made man who struggled against the greatest of odds to become a successful entrepreneur. This volume tells this story through the extraordinary life of a man one cannot help but admire. It sets the stage for his own moving account of his life. Venture's autobiography reveals him to be a man of talent and determination, as committed to American values as any of the founders, and more committed to seeing the nation fulfill its grand goal of universal human freedom and opportunity.

Venture did not live to see an end to American slavery, but by the time of his death in 1805 he had personally brought freedom to several former slaves and set an example of what they might accomplish if given the opportunity. His autobiography, published only seven years before his death, still stands as irrefutable evidence of the great American contradiction there from before the nation's existence and of the irrepressible spirit and the strong will necessary to overcome the power of socially sanctioned oppression.

Venture Smith's victory over injustice and degradation bears a vital message for societies of the 21st century. This story, lost to all but a very few Americans for more than two centuries, was brought to public life at a grand event organized by the Beecher House Center for the Study of Equal Rights in Torrington, Connecticut; the Wilberforce Institute for the study of Slavery and Emancipation (WISE) in Hull, England; and the University of Connecticut. The two-day 2006 conference was held on the Storrs campus of the university, at the Congregational Church in East Haddam where Venture Smith is buried, and at his Haddam Neck farm. The event brought the public together with some of the nation's most distinguished historians, archaeologists, geneticists, anthropologists, genealogists, poets, actors, and educators, to explore Smith's extraordinary life. Prominent among the contributors to this revolutionary project were more than a dozen of Venture Smith's descendants who spoke to the conference participants, telling the story of their ancestor from the family's perspective.

This volume then is a gift to all those who seek to understand the complex racial beginnings of America: It helps to connect the broad American story with the stories of many Americans whose lives illustrate the national struggle to live out the national ideals. The life of Venture Smith is the American story: African-American history *is* American history, made by Americans in America.

James O. Horton
Washington D.C., July 2007

"Many other interesting and curious passages of his life might have been inserted; but on account of the bulk to which they must necessarily have swelled this narrative, they were omitted."

–*The Narrative of the Life and Adventures of Venture*, New London Bee, 1798

INTRODUCTION

VOLUME II.]   WEDNESDAY, DECEMBER 26, MDCCXCVIII.   [NUMBER 72.

NEW-LONDON : PRINTED AND PUBLISHED BY CHARLES HOLT.

Just published, and for sale at this office,
PRICE 1/.
A NARRATIVE
OF THE
LIFE AND ADVENTURES
OF
VENTURE,
A native of Africa, but above sixty years an inhabitant of the United States of America.

Related by himself, and attested by respectable witnesses.

⎡Venture is a negro remarkable for size, strength, industry, fidelity, and frugality, and well known in the state of Rhode Island, on Long Island, and in Stonington, East Haddam, and several other parts of this state.
Descended from a royal race,
Benevolent and brave ;
On Afric's *savage plains* a PRINCE,
In this *free land* a SLAVE.⎦

Promotional ad for Venture's 1798 Narrative

If only Venture Smith could write.

Perhaps one should not begin the story of a remarkable man with regret. But because he was such a remarkable man, we want to know more. The core of what we know about him came from the pen of a scribe, a modest pamphlet, and a tombstone erected more than 200 years ago.

The rest has been painstakingly stitched together by recollection, research, and scholarship.

Did the schoolteacher Elisha Niles,[5] who recorded Venture's story, or the publisher Charles Holt, who printed it, or both of them, assume the role of editing his narrative in the interest of saving space? Did Venture himself avoid telling everything in order to spare his audience "the bulk?" We will never know.

Posterity can at least be grateful for the professed efforts of those who produced Venture's narrative to leave an accurate account of his life "in which nothing is added in substance to what he related himself," as the preface to the published account stated in 1798.[6] It is not what may have been added, however, but what may have been left out that gives pause. For example, there are no known images of Venture or his family, either during their lifetimes or later. We can only guess what they look like from meager written descriptions and telltale cemetery remains.

The main gift to the historical record is the compression of a full and unique life of 77 years into a narrative of fewer than 10,000 words, barely the length of a class thesis today. One cannot help but compare this with the extensive autobiography written by Smith's contemporary, the highly literate slave Gustavus Vassa (Olaudah Equiano), which is much richer in detail, observation, and context.[7]

Gustavus Vassa
(Olaudah Equiano)
front piece of his
narrative

What seems apparent from reading Venture's narrative, however, is that the paucity of information can be traced in part to the man's character as much as to the mechanics of storytelling. This was a man of action, not of words. Unlike Vassa, who garbed himself in the trappings of British society and was not above gilding his credentials, Venture most valued simplicity, frugality, and prudence. He was the kind of man who took pride in saying *"Expensive gatherings of my mates I commonly shunned, and all kinds of luxuries I was perfectly a stranger to."*

Although frustrating to historians and archaeologists, who hunger for the small details that fill in the puzzle of the past, such people do tend to tell the truth. Historians could hardly ask for more.

Another anomaly about Venture Smith's narrative is that nearly one-third of the story is given to the first decade of his life in Africa, before he evolved into the man who became a legend. For some reason, we see more detail about the African environment of his boyhood than about the land where he made his mark. There was a growing interest in things African among the English-reading public at the end of the 18th century, largely as a result of other widely published slave narratives. Charles Holt, then a savvy and ambitious

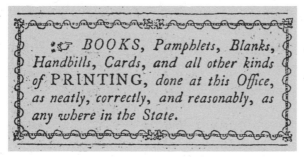

☞ BOOKS, Pamphlets, Blanks, Handbills, Cards, and all other kinds of PRINTING, done at this Office, as neatly, correctly, and reasonably, as any where in the State.

Charles Holt's front page advertisement for his printing business

26-year-old newspaper publisher from Connecticut, believed there was a market for Venture's narrative. His advertisement promoting the Narrative describes Venture: "On Afric's *savage plains* a PRINCE, in this *free land* a SLAVE."

Speculation about what may have been stressed or omitted in the recorded first-person story invariably raises the specter of a "black message in a white envelope," as scholar of slavery John Sekora described the genre of as-told-to narratives. An American slave, even a freed one, had no access to printing facilities in those days and needed white patrons to get his story published. In addition, a published narrative was often "certified" for its veracity by established members of the white community to secure its credibility. In Venture's case, five prominent residents of New London County, Connecticut, including two relatives of former owners, signed a certificate at the end of the Narrative, endorsing its substance.

The scribe Niles and his influence over Venture's story constitute another facet of this puzzle. Niles was known to have been fervently religious, although his somewhat tortured Christian obsessions[8] do not appear to have insinuated themselves into Venture's biography. Some members of Niles' family were slave owners,[9] but any enthusiasm for the institution does not show in the Narrative. In fact, commentary about religion and the institution of slavery are strangely absent from Venture's narrative.

In the end, we are persuaded for many reasons that the account is largely rendered by the subject himself, and despite possible shortcomings, it is a treasured document.

Venture's narrative opens a rare personal window on the faceless institution of slavery and offers compelling testimony to its lesser-known practice in the northern states. Add to this the extraordinary nature of the man himself, who was present at the very birth of the American nation as a self-emancipated free man, and it is no wonder that Venture Smith's life has fostered an extensive body of scholarship and inquiry.

The most focused investigation to date is the Documenting Venture Smith Project, which mobilized in 2005 a remarkable coalition of historians, archivists, anthropologists, geneticists, and civil rights activists to pursue and share research under the leadership of the Connecticut-based Beecher House Center for the Study of

Equal Rights, the Wilberforce Institute for the study of Slavery and Emancipation, in Hull, England, and the University of Connecticut. This collaboration coincided with the 200th anniversary of Venture's death.

The continuing research has been bolstered by several factors. To begin with, a great deal of scholarship has been conducted about the institution and chronology of the Atlantic slave trade, which spanned three centuries. Because slaves were treated as a commodity and the British were meticulous in keeping track of their business transactions, the record of slavery in the colonies was voluminous, and, at least in dry financial vernacular, quite precise. Thanks to the historical preservation communities in Britain, the United States, and the West Indies, these records have been retained and made available for study.

Annual wreath-laying by Venture Smith descendants at East Haddam gravesite on September 23, 2006

Also adding immeasurably to the documentation project is a clear genealogical line from Venture to the present day. His descendants not only live, but care. Some of them, who reside in his adopted state of Connecticut, have given their approval, time, memories, and correspondence to this effort.

Advances in DNA technology have also been brought to bear to determine Venture's origins and the environment in which northern

Introduction

slavery existed in the 18th century.

Because of such allies, much can be added to one man's brief narrative.

Before reviewing Venture's life journey, for much of which we have his own voice to thank, we should note that there are details of time and place in his narrative that are open to interpretation.

Venture's account is not questioned, at least by legitimate scholars, for any lack of truthfulness. No one could read his story without being persuaded that he was a man lacking in both guile and self-aggrandizement. But the written account varies in precision in several respects for what we believe are understandable reasons. First, Venture related his life story more than half a century after leaving Africa. Not only can memory be skewed by time, but the aged narrator revealed himself to be blind and wracked with pain during the telling.

Second, neither Venture nor his scribe had access to the shipping records, customhouse data, or other references that we do today.

Moreover, there is the transcription problem. When the narrator said Venture was born in "*Dukandarra*," a place found on no map, can one be sure that Niles, an unworldly country schoolteacher, wrote it down correctly? There is no evidence that Venture, who called himself "*illiterate*," could read or write, so he could hardly have helped with spelling.

But the biggest conundrum has to do with dates. Venture said he "*had completed my eighth year*" when first arriving in America. Recent investigation, based on ships' logs, custom house records, and verifiable names supplied by Venture himself, strongly suggests he was 11 or 12 — or at the very least 10 at the time. It is important to keep in mind that the culture from which he came may have operated with different measurements of time. But for the purposes of this modern-day interpretation, knowing his age is vital to matching the progression of his life against known historical events and dates.

Interestingly, the reconciliation of the dates in Venture's narrative and those in the historical record ironed itself out with time. His own estimate of being 69 years old when he dictated his story in 1798 conforms closely with verified information.

Last, the Narrative said Venture was born with the name "Broteer Furro." Like everything else about this man, his name has been put under a scholar's microscope, and interpretations will be discussed for years to come.

For the most part, we have spared the general reader the details of these sometimes conflicting ruminations in order to tell, without undue interruption, the story of an extraordinary man who lived in extraordinary times.

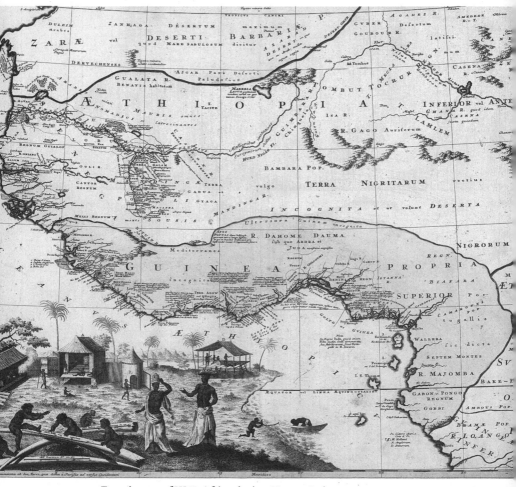

1743 French map of West Africa during Venture's time

"They seize . . . even nobles, sons of nobles,
even the members of our own family."

–AFONSO, king of Congo, to the king of Portugal, 1526

THE EARLY YEARS

Venture Smith's narrative opens with his birth, which he estimated was *about the year 1729,* the first son of a wealthy prince in
West Africa.

Although he did not mention his specific ethnicity, it is known he
came from a cattle-herding people from the interior of West Africa.
"*I descended from a very large, tall and stout race of beings, much larger than
the generality of people in other parts of the globe,*" Venture said, a description that fit his own adult dimensions.

He said the place of his birth was "*Dukandarra, in Guinea,*" a geo-
graphic term that served at the time to include a broad area of West
Africa.   Guinea in the early 18th century was almost four times the
size of America's 13 colonies and had not yet been divided into the
dozen or so European colonies that would eventually emerge as independent nations in the 20th century.

Three modern-day countries have adopted the name — Guinea,
Guinea-Bissau, and Equatorial Guinea — but together they constitute
only about ten percent of the former territory.

Suffice it to say that Venture came from the hinterland of West
Africa's so-called Gold Coast, an area rich in wildlife and vegetation,
with plentiful savanna grasslands for raising cattle and sheep.

The earliest event "*worthy of notice*" in the young boy's life was a
disagreement between his mother and father, Saungm Furro, over the
father taking a third wife without her consent, which was against custom. His mother was so upset, she took her three children and left.

As Venture recalled:

> *She took not the least sustenance along with her, to support either herself or children. I was able to travel along by her side; the other two of her offspring she carried one on her back, and the other being a sucking child, in her arms. When we became hungry, my mother used to set us down on the ground, and gather some of the fruits which grew spontaneously in that climate. These served us for food on the way. At night we all lay down together in the most secure place we could find, and reposed ourselves until morning. Though there were many noxious animals there; yet so kind was our Almighty protector, that none of them were ever permitted to hurt or molest us.*

They traveled eastward for a week, taking five days to cross a *"great desert,"* until they reached an area of fertile plains. There, his mother left him in the care of a rich farmer and set out *"for her own country,"* which was not defined, presumably with her two youngest children. It was common practice for a noble son to be apprenticed

The Savannah in modern-day Ghana

with a trusted elder to prepare him for future leadership. This is likely what the boy's mother had in mind when she left him in the man's care.

The boy was put to work tending sheep. Unbeknownst to him,

this would prove to be valuable training later in his life. Every day, he would, in the company of another boy, herd a flock of about 40 sheep to pasture two or three miles away and return at night.

Venture remembered a searing event during this early period of his life:

> *One incident which befel me when I was driving my flock from pasture, was so dreadful to me in that age, and is to this time so fresh in my memory, that I cannot help noticing it in this place. Two large dogs sallied out of a certain house and set upon me. One of them took me by the arm, and the other by the thigh, and before their master could come and relieve me, they lacerated my flesh to such a degree, that the scars are very visible to the present day.*

The guardian was sent for and carried the boy back to his place, where Broteer recuperated. The young apprentice resumed his chores until his father sent a man on a horse for him, and he returned home. Venture guessed that he had spent about a year away.

Back in his parents' home, he discovered that his mother had already come back and had reconciled with her husband. "*On my return, I was received both by my father and mother with great joy and affection, and was once more restored to my paternal dwelling in peace and happiness.*"

It would be a long time before that boy had reason to smile again.

Venture variously described his father as both a prince and a king. While his lineage may well have been long and distinguished, Saungm Furro was probably more akin to a village chieftain presiding over a generous amount of territory where his herding people could roam. His wealth was in cattle, sheep, and horses, and it was common for a man in his position to own slaves. Wealthy men also tended to amass gold, various currencies used at the time, and cowry shells, a popular form of money imported by Arab traders from Indian Ocean beaches.

Chief Furro was clearly not prepared for what was to come.

Much of West Africa in the first half of the 1700s was contested territory. The colonial powers of Europe were already active in the region, trading along the coast in slaves, guns, and other commodities, while the interior was being fought over by warring African nations seeking to expand their empires.

Shortly after young Broteer returned home, his father received word that a large army "*from a nation not far distant, furnished with musical instruments and all kinds of arms then in use*" had invaded that same area where the boy had come from, less than 150 miles away.

The peaceful agrarian people under siege sought sanctuary in Chief Furro's dominion. Being "*a kind and merciful prince,*" he readily agreed. But almost before his messenger could relay the acceptance, the people had already fled into his territory. His father gave them "*every privilege and all the protection his government could afford.*" But when they heard the enemy army was headed in their direction, the refugees fled south.

Then, Venture recalled:

> *Two days after their retreat, the report turned out to be but too true. A detachment from the enemy came to my father and informed him, that the whole army was encamped not far out of his dominions, and would invade the territory and deprive his people of their liberties and rights, if he did not comply with the following terms. These were to pay them a large sum of money, three hundred fat cattle, and a great number of goats, sheep, asses, &c.*

My father told the messenger he would comply rather than that his subjects should be deprived of their rights and privileges, which he was not then in circumstances to defend from so sudden an invasion. Upon turning out those articles, the enemy pledged their faith and honor that they would not attack him. On these he relied and therefore thought it unnecessary to be on his guard against the enemy. But their pledges of faith and honor proved no better than those of other unprincipled hostile nations.

The chief had gotten word from a reliable informant that the enemy army, while expressing satisfaction with the tribute he had paid, was in fact secretly planning to attack. He was advised to flee.

Around daybreak, the chief spirited his family out of their village and headed for a shrub plain *"some distance off."* While they rested there, smoke from a cooking fire gave away their position to an enemy scouting party. Chief Furro fired arrows at them.

This was what I first saw, and it alarmed both me and the women, who being unable to make any resistance, immediately betook ourselves to the tall thick reeds not far off, and left the old king to fight alone. For some time I beheld him from the reeds defending himself with great courage and firmness, till at last he was obliged to surrender himself into their hands.

The warriors found the family hiding. They hit Broteer on the head with a gun and put a rope around his neck. He and the women were led to the nearby army camp where his father was being held *"pinioned and haltered."* It is not known what happened to Broteer's younger brothers, Cundazo and Soozaduka, but it is presumed they were safeguarded elsewhere.

When telling this story some 60 years later, Venture said the events that followed remained vivid in his mind throughout his life, *"and I have often been overcome while thinking on it"*:

The women and myself being pretty submissive, had tolerable treatment from the enemy, while my father was closely interrogated respecting his money which they knew he must have. But as he gave them no account of it, he was instantly cut and pounded on his body with great inhumanity, that he might be induced by the torture he suffered to make the discovery. All this availed not in the least to make him give up his money, but he despised all the tortures which they inflicted, until the continued exercise and increase of torment, obliged him to sink and expire. He thus died without informing his enemies of the place where his money lay. I saw him while he was thus tortured to death.

In retrospect, one might wonder why the chief would surrender his life so painfully to save his wealth. Perhaps he knew that he would not be spared, even if he revealed the hiding place. But, more importantly, his honor and even his very identity as a leader were at stake in keeping his fortune from the hands of the enemy.

The effect of his father's resistance and death, and his being witness to both, cannot be overestimated when examining Venture Smith's later life and the shaping of his character.

The boy and women were taken prisoner by elements of an army he estimated to be about 6,000 strong. They marched west toward the sea, laying waste to the countryside and capturing everyone they could along the way.

An 18th-century French explorer, the Chevalier des Marchais, wrote that some armies in the West African interior announced their attacks "with overpowering noise, including shouting, drumming, the beating of gongs, and gunfire,"[10] a description similar to Venture's account. Like the drums and bagpipes used by colonial armies, such loud announcements served to inspire one's fighters and intimidate an enemy.

During the march, covering a distance the young Broteer estimated to be about 400 miles, he was forced to serve his captors and act as bearer. "*I was obliged to carry on my head a large flat stone used for grinding our corn, weighing as I should suppose, as much as 25 pounds; besides victuals, mat and cooking utensils.*"

Late 18th-century illustration of African slavers with captives

Venture believed he was about six-and-a-half years old at the time, although "*pretty large and stout of my age.*" Given the level of detail he observed on the march, the weight of his load, and records of later events, Venture was probably at the time at least nine or ten.[11]

THE EARLY YEARS

Historians estimate he was captured sometime between late 1738 and early 1739.

After more victorious skirmishes, in which the army collected more captives, they finally reached the sea near the port of Anomabu[12] in the middle of the Gold Coast, the preferred departure point for New England slave ships in what is present-day Ghana.

Slave castle still standing today on the Anomabu Coast

Here, the inhabitants took advantage of the arriving army's depleted strength and provisions and counterattacked, seizing its prisoners. It is not mentioned who the boy's new captors were, but they were not inclined to let a valuable commodity go free.

Slave dungeon
at Anomabu

"*I was then taken a second time,*" Venture said, and thrown into a castle where he was "*kept for market.*" The narrative does not name the castle, but the Anomabu district was infamous for its string of coastal fortresses that were used as human vaults, holding slaves for transport to Europe and the colonies. Broteer was probably held in one of the coastal castles east of Anomabu.

Given the distance and terrain covered from the point of capture to the coast, the forced march took approximately three months. Broteer likely spent another two months locked up in a portside castle.

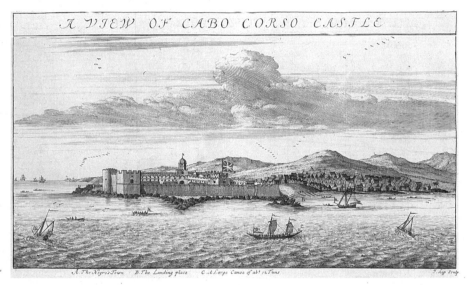

18th-century engraving of Cape Coast Castle near Anomabu

It should be noted here that Venture's narrative does not answer a number of questions, such as his birthplace, his ethnicity, or the route his captors took to the coast. Scholars continue to search for these answers.

Records of the period indicate that from 1736 to 1744 captives were first taken by small boat from a slave castle to an intermediary British ship, the *Argyle,* anchored permanently in the bay off the Anomabu coast.[13] There, slave ship captains would often make their final purchase of human cargo, completing their rosters of men, women, boys, and girls.

The young ones were particularly prized as apprentices in New England, and ship's officers often paid for them out of their own pockets as personal investments.

Broteer was rowed out to a ship called the *Charming Susanna* from Rhode Island.[14]

I was bought on board by one Robertson Mumford, steward of said vessel, for four gallons of rum, and a piece of calico, and called VENTURE, on account of his having purchased me with his own private venture. Thus I came by my name.

Mumford, whose actual given name was Robinson, evidently thought it clever to label his new acquisition for what he thought it was — a smart commercial transaction.

Four gallons of rum and a piece of calico. The price was indeed a good one by the standards of the time. An adult male in his prime could go for 100 or more gallons of rum, which was the favored currency of Rhode Island slavers.[15]

And so began the saga of an American slave.

The *Charming Susanna* embarked from the Gold Coast late in May 1739, destined for Barbados.[16] This was a typical route at the time in what came to be known as the "Triangular Trade."

Colonial ships, mainly sloops,[17] sailed from American ports to West Africa, purchased captive Africans with rum, tobacco, textiles, and guns, and then returned home by way of the West Indies. There they sold their human cargo and used the proceeds to load up with molasses and raw sugar to resupply New England's abundant distilleries.

Boston lighthouse and an armed sloop in 1729

Meanwhile, New England exported livestock, lumber, and foodstuffs to the West Indies to support what was by far Britain's most lucrative plantation economy at the time. The whole circuit was a very symbiotic arrangement.

The round trip from New England to Africa to the West Indies and home again usually took from 8 to 14 months, depending on weather and the length of time spent in ports. In the 18th century, the average duration of a slaver's voyage from the Gold Coast of West

THE EARLY YEARS

Africa to Barbados was 74 days.[18]

Venture unknowingly was near the crest of a historic surge in African slave traffic. Until 1741, 70 percent of slaves exported to the New England colonies came from the Caribbean and only 30 percent shipped directly from Africa. After that time the numbers were reversed.[19] There were many reasons for this, most having to do with the increased demand for labor and the high profit margins slavers could get from buying directly at the source. But there was also a perception among mainland slave owners that blacks raised in the West had picked up some dangerous notions of independence. Better to get them fresh from their homeland.

The *Charming Susanna* arrived in Barbados, the easternmost Caribbean island, on August 23, 1739.[20]

Bridgetown harbor, Barbados by John Waller

A sidelight: By remarkable coincidence, August 23 is recognized today by the United Nations as the "International Day for the Remembrance of the Slave Trade and Its Abolition." That date, commemorates the start of the 1791 slave revolt in the Caribbean colony of St. Domingue, now known as Haiti.

But all that took place 52 years after the West African boy peered over the ship's railing in the harbor at Bridgetown, the Barbadian capital.

In his narrative, Venture said little about the transatlantic voyage, except to estimate that about one-quarter of the captives died of smallpox before arriving in Barbados.

Perhaps he blocked out the horror of it. Other eyewitness accounts of the infamous "Middle Passage," as the transatlantic slave voyages were called, evoked a veritable hell at sea.

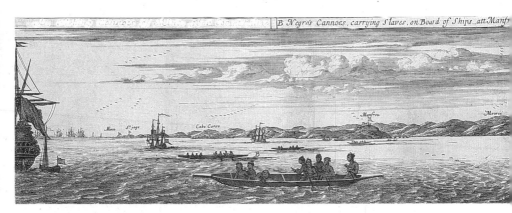

Slaves being rowed out to a slave ship on the coast near Anomabu

Captives were usually brought out to the ship from the African shore in small numbers under guard to reduce their chances of escape, but sometimes the rowboats capsized in rough water or during a skirmish with the crew.

Once aboard ship, the slaves were often stripped and branded with a hot iron, if they had not already been branded onshore, so that owners would later be able to identify their property.

When the ship got under way, panic often broke out as the captives realized they were being taken from their homeland, and bringing them to heel resulted in more casualties among both slaves and sailors.

When it became clear to the captives that resistance was futile, a "fixed melancholy," the loss of desire to live, overcame many of them.[21] Some resisted by refusing to eat, but were force-fed by the crew. Slaving captains knew that their cargo was valuable only if delivered alive, and they had to balance that reality against the temptation to pack their ships as fully as possible.

The women and children were locked away in a separate bulkhead from the men. Men were kept in the hold of the ship, which was dark and so fetid from body heat and waste that it was difficult to breathe. Chained together on double-decked wooden pallets, they had less than two feet of head room and could hardly move, except when thrown against each other in rough weather.

Slaves were also kept in the dark as to their fate. When the British slave Olaudah Equiano remembered being taken aboard ship as a boy, "I asked if we were not to be eaten by those white men with horrible looks, red faces and long hair?"[22]

In order to reduce the threat of disease and atrophy, the slaves were periodically brought on deck for exercise, fresh air, and to be bathed.

It has been calculated from departure and arrival records spanning more than two centuries that 17.4 percent of slaves died during the "Middle Passage" as a result of storms, disease, infection, or suicide, or at the hands of the crew. Losses among crewmen were considerable, although seldom as high. They called the West African voyage "The White Man's Grave."[23] It is known that at least two of the *Charming Susanna* officers died at sea on later voyages, both of them Mumfords.[24]

Venture was one of the majority on his ship to survive the experience. According to British customs' records, 78 of the estimated 91 slaves aboard the *Charming Susanna* actually made it to Barbados.[25] All but four were sold on the island. Because Venture belonged to the Rhode Island ship's steward, the boy stayed aboard.

As the Caribbean island closest to Africa, Barbados was the first stop—a throbbing economic powerhouse, studded with plantations that produced the "white gold" so coveted by Britain and its minions. The economy in Barbados and throughout the West Indies was totally dependent on enslaved Africans, who worked from morning to night to harvest and process sugar cane under the most oppressive heat and working conditions.

Loading sugar hogsheads in the West Indies in the 18th-century

As an African, the ship-bound boy might have gazed wistfully at the tropical port, with its swaying palms, stately buildings, and the distant sugar plantations, which may have looked idyllic from afar.

What he could not have known was that Barbados, Jamaica, Hispaniola, and other such Caribbean islands were unsurpassed as slave killing fields.

A telling fact: To replace their rapidly dying workers, the West Indies imported more slaves from Africa during the 17th and 18th centuries than did the entire North American continent. Barbados alone imported almost 435,000 slaves from Africa, compared with an estimated 455,000 brought to the North American mainland over the lifetime of the Atlantic slave trade.[26]

Venture may have been headed for an unfamiliar environment in the north, but his chances of surviving and shaping his own destiny there would be far greater than ever possible in Barbados.

The *Charming Susanna* arrived in Rhode Island sometime in September 1739, after what Venture's narrative described as a *"comfortable passage."*

In contrast to the Atlantic voyage, during which he was confined, the boy may have had the run of the ship on that final leg and was probably well fed on the newly provisioned vessel by a greatly relaxed crew relieved to be going home.

On arrival in Rhode Island, Robinson placed Venture with one of his sisters before bringing him later to the family's main residence on Fishers Island in Long Island Sound.

The Mumfords were a comparatively prosperous family that first settled in Rhode Island in the 1630s. Within half a century, Mumford men were heavily engaged in the international slave trade and in managing farms and plantations with slave labor. There was even a city called Mumfort on Africa's Gold Coast, near where Broteer was held for transport.[27]

One can only imagine the depth of bewilderment felt by this young African. He presumably spoke no English, was likely experiencing an unwelcome chill from the New England autumn, and had not the slightest idea how to comport himself in a bustling, foreign culture.

Slaves just off the ship often arrived weakened and disoriented, and some did not survive the transition. But Venture was young, robust, and resourceful, and his narrative makes no mention of any particular difficulties.

He arrived at a time when it was no longer a novelty to see a black African on a New England street, although it was not nearly as commonplace as it would become in another decade. Between 1720 and 1750, the slave population of Rhode Island multiplied more than sixfold.[28]

New England, however, never achieved the status of a "slave society," as did the South. Enslaved African labor became the primary engine of the southern economy, while in the mid-18th century the North depended on a labor force comprised of Africans, Native Americans, indentured servants from Britain and Europe, and its own sons and daughters to get the job done. African slaves were the lowest in this hierarchy and often suffered at the hands of resentful white laborers.

Although Venture was probably unaware of it, the year after he arrived in America, Virginia passed a law that defined its slaves as "chattel personal in the hands of their owners and possessors for all intents, construction, and purpose whatsoever."[29] By virtue of their greater diversity, the northern states may not have defined the institution of slavery quite so strictly, but in the mid-1700s, New England was far from a place of refuge.

The institution of slavery was widely accepted in the North as a means of filling a growing demand for manual labor. Although some in the New England establishment opposed slavery on moral grounds, abolition would not enter mainstream social thought in the North for nearly another century.

Venture stayed for "*some time*" with one of Robinson Mumford's married sisters — most likely his eldest, Mercy, who lived in Newport. It is presumed that Robinson wanted Venture to spend his early days with his sister because she could teach the boy how to speak rudimentary English, how to perform household chores, and, in general, how to behave in "proper" colonial society.

Sometime in 1740, the young slave was retrieved and taken to his owner's home on Fishers Island. Immediately south of the Connecticut mainland, Fishers Island had become the base for the Mumford family branch headed at the time by Capt. George Mumford, Robinson's father. But they did not own it. They leased it from relatives, the Winthrops, who constituted one of the most prominent New England families, producing governors in both Connecticut and Massachusetts.

Indeed, the Mumford clan pointedly did not amass its own property in the 18th century, but rather acted as itinerant agents, brokers, and managers for others. In effect, the array of Mumford enterprises, ranging from New England to Africa to the West Indies, served as an

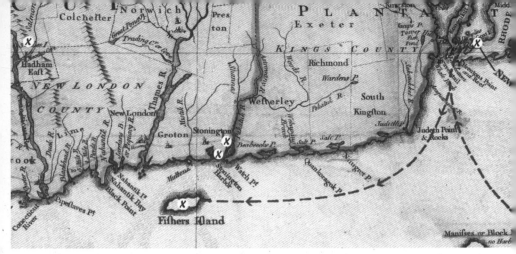

Connecticut and Rhode Island coast, including Fishers Island

18th-century version of "one-stop shopping" for those who needed ships, slaves, and provisions for the triangular trade.

As Venture would soon learn, the 2,600-acre Fishers Island played a significant role in the slave economy, part of the crucial breadbasket for the Caribbean sugar plantations.

But first the young slave had some adjustment issues. Shortly after arriving on the island Venture faced his first real test as a captive servant.

As Venture described the incident in his narrative, Robinson sent him ahead to the island while his owner took care of business on the mainland, and had turned over the keys of his ship's trunks to the boy, with instructions "*not to deliver them up to any body, not even to his father without his orders.*"

Evidently Robinson suspected that members of his family would pry. Indeed, his father tried.

He insisted that I should deliver to him the keys, threatening to punish me if I did not. But I let him know that he should not have them let him say what he would. He then laid aside trying to get them. But notwithstanding he appeared to give up trying to obtain them from me, yet I mistrusted that he would take some time when I was off my guard, either in the day time or at night to get them, therefore I slung them round my neck, and in the day time concealed them in my bosom, and at night I always lay with them under me, that no person might take them from me without being apprized of it. Thus I kept the keys from every body until my master came home. When he returned he asked where VENTURE was. As I was then within hearing, I came, and said, here sir, at your service. He asked me for his keys, and I immediately took them off my neck and reached them out to him. He took them, stroked my hair, and commended me, saying in presence of his father that his young VENTURE was so faithful that he never would have been able to have taken the keys from him but by violence; that he should not fear to trust him with his whole fortune, for that he had been in his native place so habituated to keeping his word, that he would sacrifice even his life to maintain it.

Robinson Mumford realized that he had found a gem forged by African traditions of honor. What he likely did not know was that the boy's searing memory of his father's death reinforced such tenaciousness and would become the adult's hallmark.

Initially, young Venture was put to work in the Mumford household carding wool and performing other domestic chores. Because he was big and strong for his age, he was eventually assigned to work outdoors.

Fishers Island was primarily used for grazing when the Mumfords leased it. At any given time, they raised from 1,000 to 2,000 sheep and up to 300 beef and dairy cattle (Joshua Hempstead reported in his *Diary* for Tuesday, April 6, 1731, that in an inventory of livestock that he conducted for the Winthrops, he "counted out 1350 Sheep and 42 Cows and 20 Swine 16 of them Sows and 1 Boar 8 Mares with foal 4 oxen &c").[30] The island was a major meat supplier, and the Mumfords paid their cousins the Winthrops 1,100 pounds a year, a staggering amount at the time, for the privilege of using it.[31]

The Mumfords also had a long-standing history of slaveholding. George's mother had even been murdered on the Rhode Island mainland by a slave in 1707.

The incident served as an example of how slave crimes were dealt with. Abigail Mumford had ordered her slave whipped. He turned on her and beat her to death. When he realized he could not escape capture, he drowned himself in Narragansett Bay. The citizens were so outraged at being deprived of their retribution, the Rhode Island Assembly ordered the dead slave's head, arms, and legs be cut from his body and hung in public view, and his torso burned to ashes "that it may, if it pleased God, be something of a terror to others from perpetrating of the like barbarity for the future."[32]

Since it was an ingrained family legend, the new boy called Venture must have heard the story as he adjusted to life as a slave in the Mumford household.

Islands like Fishers were ideal for raising livestock, because they were protected from one of the great scourges of the time — wolves. Packs of them had roamed the Northeast with impunity and cut heavily into livestock herds on the mainland before they were hunted out by the mid-18th century. As testimony to their importance as refuges for sheep, no fewer than five "Ram" islands could be found along the

Connecticut and Long Island coasts.

All the islands in the Long Island basin, whose owners had been given special status by the crown as "Lords of the Manor," were similarly mobilized. Between them, they served as a major provisioning source for the Caribbean sugar plantations, and later, for the soldiers fighting in the War of Independence. By 1750, the area had become the North's major livestock exporter, the equivalent of the Iowa beef empire in later times.

The boy was already well suited for herding work, having come from such a culture in Africa, with an apprenticeship already served. Whether his owner was aware of this when he purchased Venture is not known, but it certainly added to the boy's value.

Their relationship was to be short lived. Within two years after Venture's arrival, Robinson died, apparently at sea. His father, George, became the slave's owner and the one Venture now called "*master.*"

Initially, the old man, himself a former sea captain, was wary of his new charge, remembering the incident over the ship's trunks and perhaps the fate of his mother. But Venture's formidable work ethic eventually won him over. Venture said Mumford began to put more confidence in him "*after many proofs of my faithfulness.*" Venture described his demeanor in those days as obedient and submissive, but it would soon be shaken. The old man started imposing harder and harder tasks on the boy, such as forcing him to pound bushels of corn for the chickens late into the night "*or be rigorously punished.*"

He then faced a new problem that was not uncommon in the slave culture — serving two masters. In this case, Mumford's eldest son, James, the late Robinson's brother, evidently took pleasure in flexing his authority. When the old man was away, James would order Venture to do chores that were different from those the father assigned. The young slave quietly complied, until one day:

> . . . *his son came up to me in the course of the day, big with authority, and commanded me very arrogantly to quit my present business and go*

directly about what he should order me. I replied to him that my master had given me so much to perform that day, and that I must therefore faithfully complete it in that time. He then broke out into a great rage, snatched a pitchfork and went to lay me over the head therewith; but I as soon got another and defended myself with it, or otherwise he might have murdered me in his outrage. He immediately called some people who were within hearing at work for him, and ordered them to take his hair rope and come and bind me with it. They all tried to bind me but in vain, tho' there were three assistants in number. My upstart master then desisted, put his pocket handkerchief before his eyes and went home with a design to tell his mother of the struggle with young VENTURE. He told her that their young VENTURE had become so stubborn that he could not control him, and asked her what he should do with him. In the mean time I recovered my temper, voluntarily caused myself to be bound by the same men who tried in vain before, and carried before my young master, that he might do what he pleased with me. He took me to a gallows made for the purpose of hanging cattle on, and suspended me on it. Afterwards he ordered one of his hands to go to the peach orchard and cut him three dozen of whips to punish me with. These were brought to him, and that was all that was done with them, as I was released and went to work after hanging on the gallows about an hour.

This incident showed Venture what bondage was all about, and he took from it some lessons. First he behaved submissively, but found he could be jolted into rage by an oppressor. He also learned that he could physically handle himself well, even with three grown men. But when his rage cooled, he surrendered himself back into submission.

In retrospect, one wonders what else an intelligent young man with an urge to live could have done on an island in an unfamiliar land. He took his punishment.

But this early affair in his slave life may well have been the spark that ignited Venture Smith's determination to become his own man. From then on, he bided his time and learned the ways of the owner class.

Daily life for a slave in a New England household was quite different in texture from that of a southern plantation slave; the environment and the type of work were so different in the two regions. While much of the southern and mid-Atlantic colonies was flat and fertile, ideal for the growing of large crops, rocky and hilly New England could mostly sustain small farms with a small number of slaves.

The two economies had not yet been joined by the collaboration of raw cotton and the textile mills powered by New England's fast-

1771 price list for goods sold in the West Indies (see note 33 for transcription)

moving rivers. Eli Whitney did not invent the cotton gin until the end of the century.

As testimony, however, to the North's growing role as a major supplier for the Caribbean sugar-growing slave population, a number of spacious farms emerged in the Narragansett area flatlands of Rhode Island, in the Manor Islands of Long Island Sound, in eastern Connecticut, and the Dutch plantations of the Hudson Valley. All of them used slave labor in the 18th century to raise sheep, beef cattle, dairy cows, and horses as well to as grow the foodstuffs that were shipped to the West Indies.[33]

Northern supplies weren't just for the sustenance of overworked slaves in the West Indies, of course, but for the white owners and managers who pampered themselves in typical British colonial style. Among the items that Connecticut plantations were known to have shipped south were trotting horses and massive quantities of ice.

Timber, especially the white oak prized by New England shipyards, was also a precious northern commodity shipped south to make the barrels that carried sugar and molasses on the return trip north.

Venture spoke little of his surroundings on Fishers Island, where he probably shared quarters with over 20 other slaves needed to operate a vast livestock enterprise. Because most northern farms were smaller, slaves were usually not housed in outside barracks-like quarters, as in the South. They would usually live in the attic or basement of the main house, in cramped and Spartan conditions, or in a nearby barn. In the winter, some of the men would sleep in the kitchen and hallways inside a bedroll, with the task of keeping the fires burning through the night.

Such proximity to owners did not necessarily foster racial cohesion in the North. A family's slaves may have lived in the main house but were not allowed to use the front entrance, for example. They entered and left through the "slave door," which usually adjoined the kitchen. They also had a separate outhouse, far removed from the one used by the whites.

Instead of the southern field hand's monotonous routine of tending and picking crops like tobacco in Virginia or rice in Georgia from dawn to dusk, a northern slave usually had a variety of chores. Depending on the need of the moment, he might work in the field in the morning and the shop in the afternoon. The standard tasks for male slaves included chopping wood, repair work of all kinds, shoeing horses, making bricks, mucking out stalls, feeding livestock, or plowing and sowing. In the evening, slaves might polish boots, crush grain for the poultry, and keep the fireplace stoked.

In the provisioning trades, a black man could work alone — minding and herding stock, loading and driving wagons, or running a fishing boat. He was judged by the results at the end of the day and could well face a whipping if the job was not done to his owner's satisfaction.

Female slaves in a middle-class household usually worked indoors — mostly cooking, laundering, and cleaning — and as dairy maids in the barn. In the evening, they would work in the kitchen, cleaning up after dinner and preparing the next day's meals or sewing and darning their owners' clothes.

On small subsistence farms, slaves often worked side by side with their owners to get the daily job done. They might normally work in comfort together, but there was a social line one seldom crossed. Not learning it carried a price.

One might think that the proximity of master and slave in the North encouraged more tolerance and kindness than in the South, where the demands of massive crop production for a hungry world more greatly pressed its slaves. But as Ira Berlin noted in his seminal work on the first two centuries of slavery in North America, *Many Thousands Gone*, just the opposite often proved true: "Slaveholders in such societies could act with extraordinary brutality precisely because their slaves were extraneous to their main business. They could limit their slaves' access to freedom expressly because they desired to set themselves apart from their slaves."[34]

Berlin and other historians have also noted that the system of mixed living in the North had a profound impact on slave family life and connectedness to their heritage. The absence of separate slave quarters not only broke up family units but hastened the dissolution of the African communal structure. As a result, northern slaves were less able than their southern counterparts to practice their African religions or preserve ancient traditions and adapt them in any cohesive way to their new conditions and environment.

On the other hand, because their work ran the full gamut of maintaining hearth to economy in the North, slaves there tended to develop skills that could serve them well in independence. Few got the opportunity to prove that.

Venture spent the first 15 years of his slave life in the keep of the Mumfords on Fishers Island.

Fishers Island in 1762 by Ezra Stiles

The seven-mile-long island, tucked away between the eastern tip of Long Island and the Connecticut mainland, bears a passing resemblance to a fish swimming westward, with a small harbor cut behind its head. A map hand drawn by Ezra Stiles and dated 1762 shows only one dwelling near the harbor and a few patches of forest. Interestingly, the map's legend mentions 50 deer in residence but makes no mention of livestock or slaves.

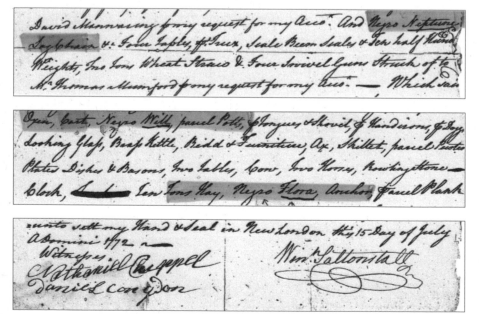

New London auction sale 1772, signed by Winthrop Saltenstall

This was not uncommon. Property bills of sale at the time often lumped together household goods, animals, and slaves.[35]

The privileged Winthrops behaved like the English landed gentry from the Old Country. They even kept a herd of albino deer on Naushon, one of the Elizabeth Islands, off the southern coast of Massachusetts.

Venture's skills as a woodsman, herder, builder, and fisherman were honed here. It is not known if he hunted. Slaves were normally not allowed to use guns.

He grew to be a man of enormous size, by his own account *"measuring six feet one inch and a half, and every way well proportioned."*

There was no job he could not do, and he seemed to take pride in doing it in shorter time and in greater quantity than anyone else. Once, to test his strength, *"I took up on my knees a tierce of salt containing seven bushels, and carried it two or three rods. Of this fact there are several eye witnesses now living,"* he told his biographer a half century later. Translated into modern measurements, the young man had carried a weight of nearly 500 pounds a distance of approximately 40 feet.

Occasionally he took trips to the Connecticut and Rhode Island mainland, less than an hour north by small boat, in the company of George or James, to deliver wood or produce. He also made deliveries to the eastern end of Long Island, 18 miles south.

Port towns like Groton, New London, and Stonington in Connecticut and Westerly in Rhode Island were the only populated places he would experience in those formative years. It is not known how much he learned of the wider world at the time.

For example, he might have heard something through the slave network about an insurrection in New York City in 1741 that newspapers of the time labeled a "Negro Conspiracy." Although it was not a slave revolt, the incident served as a horrendous example of explosive race relations in the growing cities. A series of building fires had set off mass hysteria, and scores of blacks were rounded up as suspects. A total of 31 were executed. Some were burned at the stake and others were hanged. Interestingly, whites were also implicated in this so-called plot, and five of them were hanged.[36] These were mostly Irish immigrants, whom the English colonists labeled a separate "race" in those days.

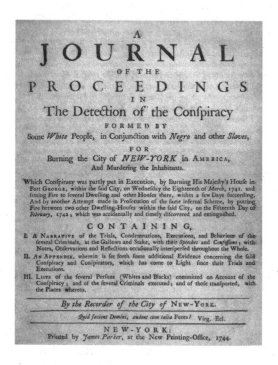

1744 report on the
New York riots

Of an even wider world, Venture might have overheard something about "King George's War," as the third French and Indian war was called. Mostly centered in upper New York and Canada, the war was physically distant, but it nevertheless wielded an indirect impact. Blacks became more essential to the northern economy as able-bodied whites went off to join the British war effort, which would last off and on until 1763.

Venture and his people worked harder as a result, comforted by the dubious solace of knowing that their value as slaves had increased.

Coming from a culture that measured time by nature's clock, Venture must have also found it a particular curiosity that England

and her colonies, after much calculation and debate, reverted in 1752 from the Julian to the Gregorian calendar. It was an edict that prompted riots among citizens who felt cheated out of 11 days.

While Venture labored in the fields and tidewaters of an offshore island, preoccupied with his daily chores and orders, revolutionary notions about the rightness of scientific reasoning, the limitations of the divine right of kings, the equality of men, and a people's right to self-determination were swirling through the parlors and assembly halls on the colonial mainland.

What he would soon come to learn was that such notions did not apply to him.

"People might not get all they work for in this world,
but they must certainly work for all they get."

–FREDERICK DOUGLASS, August 3, 1857

THE CRUCIBLE YEARS

The year 1754 marked a turning point in Venture's life.

He was now about 26 and in the prime of his life. He had been confined to the Mumford household for a decade and a half and was bursting to expand his horizons.

Venture had clearly been planning something, for he had put aside quite a bit of money by doing odd jobs at night like polishing boots, trapping muskrats and minks, fishing, and selling vegetables he was evidently allowed to raise by himself.

This was not unusual in the right circumstances. A northern slave owner with any understanding of how to motivate servants realized that he would get good work from a man during the day if that man had the opportunity to work for himself in off-hours. And Venture was clearly a good worker. What also distinguished him was how he dealt with his money. He saved nearly everything as an investment for the future. Venture had almost an obsessive aversion to spending money on items that were not absolutely essential.

One event he was saving for was matrimony. Venture took a wife in January or February 1754. His bride, Marget, whom he called "*Meg*," was a slave in the Mumford home. Little is known about her, to the great frustration of her descendants and to scholars who at the very least want to know if she was born in Africa or America or if she was Native American. As of this writing, University of Connecticut geneticists, who retrieved a bone from her grave for DNA testing in the summer of 2006, are working on the puzzle. One fact learned from that excavation was that Meg was quite small in size. Her coffin was made for someone under five feet in height.

With her husband standing more than a foot taller and weighing three times as much, the couple must have made a striking sight.

Not long after Venture started his family, something inexplicable happened. In his own words:

> *My master owned a certain Irishman, named Heddy, who about that time formed a plan of secretly leaving his master. After he had long had this plan in meditation he suggested it to me. At first I cast a deaf ear to it, and rebuked Heddy for harboring in his mind such a rash undertaking. But after he had persuaded and much enchanted me with the prospect of gaining my freedom by such a method, I at length agreed to accompany him. Heddy next inveigled two of his fellow servants to accompany us. The place to which we designed to go was the Mississippi.*

To prepare for the escape they stole provisions — *"privately collected"* is the way the Narrative phrases it — from the Mumford larder, gathered extra clothes, sneaked out to the shore at about midnight, stole their owner's boat, and *"directed our course for the Mississippi river."*

> *We mutually confederated not to betray or desert one another on pain of death. We first steered our course for Montauk point, the east end of Long-Island. After our arrival there we landed, and Heddy and I made an incursion into the island after fresh water, while our two comrades were left at a little distance from the boat, employed at cooking.*

While no one was looking, Heddy the ringleader quietly abandoned his companions and stole off on his own by foot. When they discovered his absence, Venture asked the help of local townspeople, who sent two men after Heddy. They caught up with him in Southampton, about 10 miles away and brought him back. Venture continued the story:

> *I then thought it might afford some chance for my freedom, or at least a palliation for my running away, to return Heddy immediately to his*

*master, and inform him that I was induced to go away by Heddy's
address. Accordingly I set off with him and the rest of my companions for
our master's, and arrived there without any difficulty. I informed my
master that Heddy was the ringleader of our revolt, and that he had used
us ill. He immediately put Heddy into custody, and myself and companions were received and went to work as usual.*

Although the story cries for explanations, we learn no more,
except that Heddy ended up in jail.

It is not known how much time elapsed between escape and
return, but they were gone long enough for Mumford to publish an
advertisement in a New York newspaper, offering a reward for their
return. It was one of hundreds of fugitive slave notices to be found in
northern newspapers in any given year. The ad appeared in *The New-
York Gazette* on April 1, 1754, and began: "Run away from George
Mumford, of Fisher's Island, the 27th Instant, four Men Servants, a
white Man and three Negroes, who hath taken a large two-Mast Boat,
with a square Stern, and a large white Pine Canoe . . ."

Venture had a Ker-
sey dark colour'd Great Coat, three Kersey Jackets, two Pair
of Breeches of the same, a new Cloth colour'd Fly-Coat, with
red Shalloon Lining, a green Ratteen Jacket almost new, a trimson birded Stuff ditto, a Pair of large Oznabrigs Trowsers, a
new Felt Hat, two Pair of Shoes, one Pair new, several Pair
of Stockings; he is a very tall Fellow, 6 Feet 2 Inches high,
thick square Shoulders, large bon'd, mark'd in the Face, or
scar'd with a Knife in his own Country.

Detail from runaway ad for Venture in 1754

The man Venture called Heddy was identified as "Joseph Heday,
(who) says he is a Native of Newark in the Jerseys."

Offering a reward for their return of 20 pounds in "New-York
Currency," which would be equal to about $1,000 today, the notice

describes in detail the clothes that the fugitives were wearing or carrying and then offers the first known description of Venture: "he is a
very tall Fellow, 6 Feet 2 Inches high, thick square Shoulders, Large
bon'd, mark'd in the Face, or scar'd with a Knife in his own Country."

Replicas of Venture's clothes in 1754 runaway ad

It is telling commentary about George Mumford's relationship with Venture that in all those years he never asked his slave how he came by his facial scarring — a knife cut or ritual scarification — as a boy.

Many questions remain.

How could Venture so readily have abandoned his new wife within two months of marrying her? "Cold feet" seems an unlikely explanation for someone who believed so fervently in keeping his word and who, according to his own accounts, was devoted to this woman.

A more likely explanation is that marriage unlocked in him even a greater yearning to take charge of his life. One can imagine him telling Meg that as soon as he could establish himself as a free man he would find a way to send for her so they could live together as a family, beholden only to themselves.

Venture's naiveté evokes considerable poignancy. To think that he could reach Mississippi by sailboat from the tip of Long Island, a distance of some 1,600 miles, and that when he got there he would somehow be free was sheer folly. How he would "send" for his family later was also unclear. His long isolation on a small island had clearly deprived him of essential knowledge about the real world. Heddy evidently had no illusions, having chosen to escape as soon as he reached nearby landfall.

Venture may have heard of Mississippi as a comparative paradise with a climate more to an African's liking. It had not yet emerged as the bastion of slavery it would become prior to the Civil War. But Mississippi nevertheless was no place for a black man to roam unhindered. In those days, the French ran the Gulf region with a heavy hand and had brutally put down a slave rebellion there in 1726.

When contemplating this episode, or at least the Narrative's limited version of it, we come across the first recorded instance of Venture's vaunted code of honor being violated. Given their mutual pledge of not betraying one another "*on pain of death*," Heddy got off easily.

On the other hand, we also see a shrewdly practical, even opportunistic side to Venture. By turning over his betrayer to Mumford, Venture figured that he and his cohorts would be treated leniently. Amazingly, they were.

There are many recorded examples of slaves being severely punished for much less. And yet these three were just put back to work.

In the examination of Venture's motives, historians point to a tactic that slaves developed in the 18th century called "laying out." Knowing that an owner lived in fear of losing his investment, a slave would run away and go into hiding in order to extract concessions for better treatment in exchange for his return. A third party, usually a freed slave, would act as a go-between, taking the slave's demands back to the owner and the response back to the slave. Sometimes this worked, and sometimes it backfired if the owner did not keep his word.

Although it is not known if this tactic was part of Venture's plan, his account of the escape and return suggests some kind of deal was struck, because it seems clear he avoided punishment.

However, the master's forgiveness or reward, if that is what it was, did not last long.

At the close of that year I was sold to a Thomas Stanton, and had to be separated from my wife and one daughter, who was about one month old. He resided at Stonington-point.

Just like that. We learn he was sold and separated from his family, which by then included his first child. Why?

One can surmise that Mumford's faith in Venture's loyalty had been shaken by the escape. Perhaps it was better to sell him than to risk losing him again without getting any return. But it did not happen right away, it happened about eight months after the failed escape. There were other factors.

The Mumfords had been getting ready to relocate. Records show that George purchased a house in 1755 in New London, where he moved his family and retinue of slaves the following year. That port town on the Connecticut mainland was the home base for the extended and interrelated family of Winthrops, Saltenstalls, and Mumfords.

The lease for Fishers Island was transferred to Benjamin Brown, who came from one of the slave-trading Brown families in Rhode

Island, but not the one that funded what would later become Brown University.

George Mumford died unexpectedly in New London in 1756 at the age of 67. The probated list of his property included 19 slaves, but not Meg, Hannah, or Venture. Sometime before his death, George had transferred ownership of Venture's wife and daughter to his remaining son, James.

SOUTH VIEW OF NEW-LONDON & FORT TRUMBULL.

Looking north on the Thames River with New London in background
by J. W. Barber

Venture now resided with the Stantons in the nearby town of Stonington, then a young seaport and farming community that would later become one of New England's busiest sailing ports and whaling centers. In those days, it had a slave population almost equal to New Haven's.

Fishers Island stayed in Winthrop hands for another 108 years. First granted to future colonial Connecticut Governor John Winthrop "the Younger" in 1645 and made a Manor by the Crown in 1668,[37] the island was the subject of a long-standing border dispute between New York and Connecticut. In 1880 a two-state commission determined that the island was, in fact, part of New York. Today,

Fishers Island is home to a full-time population of nearly 300 and a summer resort for the very wealthy.

At the end of 1754 Venture had become someone else's property and moved to the mainland.

To this place I brought with me from my late master's, two johannes, three old Spanish dollars, and two thousand of coppers, besides five pounds of my wife's money... All this money amounting to near twenty-one pounds York currency, my master's brother, Robert Stanton, hired of me, for which he gave me his note.

THOMAS STANTON'S HOMESTEAD.

Thomas Stanton house in Stonington, CT, built circa 1710, lost to fire in 1967

In other words, Venture put his hard-earned savings in a white man's safekeeping and got a promissory note in return. Venture, the consummate businessman, had "*hired*"—loaned—his capital to Robert Stanton, expecting to earn interest on his money. One can wonder about the wisdom of that, but what else could a slave do when pressured by an owner? He could have hidden it, but the Stantons would have easily found out from the former owners that Venture had amassed his own money. Lying about it probably would have earned him punishment.

The amount was equal to more than a year's wages for a laborer. By today's standards, the 21 pounds would be equal to about a month's pay for an unskilled worker. Coincidentally, it is almost the same amount as the reward money Mumford had put up to get his four slaves and boat back.

At this point, Venture's narrative jumps ahead 18 months to report that his owner purchased Meg and their daughter Hannah *"for seven hundred pounds old tenor,"* equal to about 100 pounds of new currency issued in 1755.[38]

After satisfying themselves that Venture was of good value, the Stantons evidently thought it would be in everyone's best interests to reunite his family. To refuse him that could cause problems. There are many stories about how slaves resisted their owners without actually escaping or refusing to work. They could slow down, get sloppy and break things, pretend not to understand, or find any variety of ways to express their unhappiness without overtly rebelling to the point of inviting the lash or sale.

However, from what is known about Venture's personality, it is unlikely he would have played such games. It is more likely that he simply asked his master to buy his wife and daughter, persuading Stanton it would make him more productive as a slave and provide new assets to the household. Venture was developing a good head for business.

So, he got his family, and the Stantons got two new slaves. A slave couple's child was, of course, born into slavery.

At this point in the Narrative, it would be perfectly understandable if the reader starts to get a little cranky. There is much information missing. The scribe Elisha Niles seems to have served as little more than a secretary taking dictation and converting the tale into his own school-learned language. Words put in Venture's mouth, like "inveigled," were not likely to have been used by a slave without formal schooling. What education he likely received as a privileged child being raised to be a leader in his father's village in Africa would have been cut short at an early age. On the other hand, articulation and eloquence in speaking do not require literacy. Many words attributed to Venture in this first-person narrative may well have come from his own lips, especially pragmatic business terms like "procure" and "solicit."

But the frustrating issue here is that, if Niles had had any sense of the substance of what he was hearing, he would have asked for explanations. There is no evidence of it.

We do not know, for example, how much Stanton paid for Venture who by this time was garnering a reputation as a human dynamo and who had to have been regarded as a highly valuable commodity. Stanton clearly enjoyed showing off his new investment.

> *One time my master sent me two miles after a barrel of molasses, and ordered me to carry it on my shoulders. I made out to carry it all the way to my master's house.*

Such a load would have weighed nearly 300 pounds.

Venture and Meg had two more children, both sons, while they were in their late twenties. Solomon was born in 1756 and Cuff in 1758. Interestingly, Cuff's name was derived from the West African word "Kofi," meaning Friday. It was the tradition there to name children for the day of the week they were born.[39] Solomon, while of Old Testament origins, was a name also frequently used in Africa.

Much has been debated about why Venture chose to live with his given slave name and to later adopt the surname of his final owner. Time and again we see a man who was determined to be a fully vested American who nevertheless took pride in being born an African of royal birth.

One point is certain: He would have never chosen Stanton for his surname. The reason is found in the Narrative.

Sometime around 1759, five years after Venture arrived at the Stanton household, Stanton's wife, Elizabeth, had a serious quarrel with Meg while the head of the house was off hunting. Venture had been working in the barn when he heard a "*racket*" in the house, and came running to find out what it was all about. In his words:

> *When I entered the house, I found my mistress in a violent passion with my wife, for what she informed me was a mere trifle; such a small affair that I forbear to put my mistress to the shame of having it known. I earnestly requested my wife to beg pardon of her mistress for the sake of*

peace, even if she had given no just occasion for offence. But whilst I was
thus saying my mistress turned the blows which she was repeating on my
wife to me. She took down her horse-whip, and while she was glutting
her fury with it, I reached out my great black hand, raised it up and
received the blows of the whip on it which were designed for my head.
Then I immediately committed the whip to the devouring fire.

It is not known what set Elizabeth Stanton off. Whatever the cause, it apparently was not Meg's doing or at least not intentionally so. It seemed more to do with Venture's defense of Meg that unleashed their mistress' fury.

The slave culture exacerbated such outbursts. The slightest word or gesture that could be inferred as rebellion from an "inferior" could not be tolerated. This overwhelming sense of owner entitlement could not be more clearly demonstrated than when a supposedly well-bred woman undertakes for a "*mere trifle*" to punish with a horsewhip two grown adults, one of them a man almost three times her size.

Venture was seeking conciliation, not retribution. Although he may have feared the consequences of striking back, recalling the story of what happened to the slave who killed George Mumford's · mother, his words and demeanor suggested he simply wanted to cool the situation down. He knew by now what it took to function in a world that was not always rational, and was certainly not fair.

After Elizabeth's husband, Thomas, returned home, she told him about the incident — or at least her version of it. Venture said his master "*seemed to take no notice of it, and mentioned not a word about it to me.*" So, Venture and Meg went back to work, thinking the matter closed. His narrative went on:

Some days after his return, in the morning as I was putting on a log in the
fire-place, not suspecting harm from any one, I received a most violent
stroke on the crown of my head with a club two feet long and as large
round as a chair-post. This blow very badly wounded my head, and the
scar of it remains to this day. The first blow made me have my wits about

me you may suppose, for as soon as he went to renew it, I snatched the club
out of his hands and dragged him out of the door.

To end the fight, Venture turned to the law.

While Thomas Stanton called his brother Robert for help, the assaulted slave took off, carrying the bloody club to a neighboring justice of the peace. If he had lived in the South at the time, such a recourse would not have been possible, but Connecticut had enacted laws against unjustifiable abuse of slaves, and Venture knew it.

The justice of the peace seemed to be a reasonable man but chose not to take immediate action. He listened to Venture's complaint and advised him to return to the Stanton farm and then to reissue a complaint if it happened again. Venture agreed to do this, but as they were talking, the Stanton brothers rode up and angrily demanded the slave's return. The justice turned on Thomas rebuking him for treating his slave "*thus hastily and unjustly, and told him what would be the consequence if he continued the same treatment towards me,*" Venture recalled.

Thus chastised, the Stantons left for home with Venture in tow. He described what happened next:

When they had come to a bye place, they both dismounted their respective
horses, and fell to beating me with great violence. I became enraged at this
and immediately turned them both under me, laid one of them across the
other, and stamped both with my feet what I would.

Venture's strength was formidable and he could have easily killed both brothers, but he just wanted to overpower them. He did not have the advantage for long, however, because after they all returned home Stanton had a local constable and two others haul Venture off to a blacksmith's shop and handcuff him.

He was then brought to the house, where Venture said his mistress asked if he was secured. When assured that he was, Elizabeth smiled with satisfaction. "*In the midst of this content and joy, I presented myself before my mistress, shewed her my hand-cuffs, and gave her thanks for my gold rings.*"

Not only had Venture shed the submissive and obedient garb that he had worn in his early slave days, but he gave as good as he got. Enraged at such insolence, Stanton had his slave padlocked with a large ox chain.

I continued to wear the chain peaceably for two or three days, when my master asked me with contemptuous hard names whether I had not better be freed from my chains and go to work. I answered him, No. Well then, (he said to) me, I will send you to the West-Indies or banish you, for I am resolved not to keep you. I answered him I crossed the waters to come here, and I am willing to cross them to return.

Those words would set into motion another change in Venture's life, but it would be a road that took many turns before straightening out.

While he and the Stantons coexisted in cold silence, a Stonington resident by the name of Hempstead Miner came to Venture and asked if he wanted to join his household. When Venture said yes, Miner quietly advised him to act as unrepentant and discontented as possible in Stanton's presence in order to bring the sale price down. Venture did so, and it worked.

Stanton sold Venture to Miner for the remarkably low price of 56 pounds at a time when strong and healthy male slaves in their prime usually commanded much higher prices.[40]

It was the winter of 1759 and Venture was about 30 years old. He certainly must have been relieved to be free of Thomas Stanton, his cruelest owner. But he was leaving his wife and three children with Stanton and his embittered family.

Making the break all the more troubling was Robert Stanton's refusal to return the considerable money in savings that Venture had turned over to him five years earlier. Thomas had broken into Venture's trunk during their dispute and destroyed the promissory note, so Venture had no proof of the 21 pounds owed him. Prior to the Revolution in America, an unskilled laborer earned only 12 to 15 pounds per year.[41] Venture had lost more than a year's wages. The legal complications this loss could later cause, however, may have been another reason why the Stantons decided to sell their most valuable slave.

Venture then got another jolt. He learned that his new owner, Hempstead Miner, had no intention of keeping him and had not fully paid Stanton his price.

But Venture had his own secret, too. He had amassed more money of his own, evidently from doing odd jobs for people in Stonington, and this time he was not going to trust anyone else to keep it. So before leaving with Miner he buried the money, the amount of which was not specified, alongside a familiar road.

Miner took his new acquisition to Hartford, which at the time was a growing city but not yet the Connecticut capital. There he tried to sell Venture to one William Hooker. When Hooker asked the big slave whether he would accompany him to "*the German Flats,*"

Venture said no.

The area in question was in upper New York and would have taken Venture at least a three-day ride away from his family. For a man in perpetual bondage, that might as well have been California. German Flats had been the site of a massacre just two years earlier during the French and Indian wars, the news of which might also have given Venture pause.

Hooker threatened to take him anyway by bodily strapping him to his sleigh, to which Venture replied with the kind of quickness that served him well throughout his adult life.

I replied to him, that if he carried me in that manner, no person would purchase me, for it would be thought that he had a murderer for sale. After this he tried no more, and said he would not have me as a gift.

Miner then offered Venture to another Hartford man named Daniel Edwards, who did not buy the slave but paid Miner 10 pounds in a pawn deal to obtain Venture's services.

VIEW OF HARTFORD FROM THE EASTERN BANK OF CONNECTICUT RIVER.

Lithograph of Hartford by J. W. Barber

Edwards, a well-to-do urban gentleman, used Venture as a man-servant — "*his cup-bearer and waiter*" — and came to place a great deal of trust in him. This included sending Venture to the cellar to fetch wine for guests, a new level of responsibility that he, being a country fellow, regarded as a privilege. After being together for *"some time,"* Edwards asked Venture *"why my master wished to part with such an honest negro"* and did not keep him for himself. *"I replied that I could not give him the reason, unless it was to convert me into cash, and speculate with me as with other commodities."*

Venture added that he hoped it was not *"on account of my ill conduct"* that Miner did not keep him. Edwards replied that he would happily become Venture's owner himself *"if it was not unreasonable and inconvenient for me to be parted from my wife and children."*

This was one of the rare moments in the narrative when Venture held a respectful and rational conversation with a member of the owning class. But there was something else about the exchange: Here was a slave who had no compunction about saying no to a white man like Stanton or Hooker but took pride in the way he could serve another.

One senses from their relationship that Venture was testing his ability to negotiate with a white man, drawing upon his intrinsic business acumen and the need to trust the other party. He probably was encouraged by the exchange with Edwards.

Venture was not an ideologue who chose to resist the enslaving class at all times and at all costs, but a pragmatist who believed a bond could be struck with all human beings. He lived by the Golden Rule — "Do unto others as you would have them do unto you."

To this he added one conviction that had been ingrained in him by the chaos of the past year: He would not serve at the pleasure of others forever. Venture was determined to become his own man. He also knew it would not be easy, for the process of achieving one's freedom was not yet common.

There were basically three ways that a slave could gain his freedom in 18th-century New England: by escaping, then disappearing in a large city or crossing into Canada or the western frontier; through manumission, that is, being released by the owner; or by "redeeming oneself," as buying one's own freedom was called.

As he had learned six years earlier, escape was out of the question for a man who valued his family. Manumission occasionally occurred, if one was fortunate enough to be bought by someone who became disenchanted with the institution of slavery or decided to release his slaves upon his death. But freeing a slave was not as simple as it might seem.

Colonial authorities did not want to be burdened with the prospect of supporting freed slaves who were no longer regarded as productive, a social trend that was creating a welfare problem.[42] The Connecticut legislature had passed in 1702 a law that required former owners and their heirs to take financial responsibility for freed blacks if they became itinerant beggars or burdens on society.[43]

Other states had similar laws. Until 1782 Virginia, for example, would allow a slave to be manumitted only if the owner took "responsibility for the support of sick or crippled, all females under 18 and over 45 and all males under 21 and over 45."[44]

In 1723 the Rhode Island General Assembly passed a law that appeared to encourage manumission, but required the freed slave to pay one hundred pounds, in case he was unable to support himself. This financial burden made manumission extremely difficult to attain.

The consequences of this difficulty could be seen throughout the North. The ratio of slaves to free blacks rose sharply in the prerevolutionary years with the growth of industry, food production, and a professional class in search of servants. In the period leading up to the War of Independence, Connecticut had the highest number of slaves in New England. Its black population in 1774 was close to 8,000, and about 6,400 were still enslaved.[45]

Good as his word, Venture's Hartford patron furnished him with a horse so the slave could return to Stonington to visit his family. When he reached the Stanton farm, a good day's ride south, Venture reunited with Meg, whom he had probably not seen for more than a year. Before long, Thomas Stanton appeared. "*As my old master appeared much ruffled at my being there,*" Venture departed. It behooved of him not to reopen old wounds while his family remained at the mercy the Stantons.

More than ever now, Venture yearned to be near his family and wanted his status resolved. He turned his horse in the direction of Long Point in Stonington where merchant and shipbuilder Oliver Smith Jr. had recently taken up residence.

Stonington Long Point by J. W. Barber

Venture had learned that Hempstead Miner, who had still not settled with Stanton, had already given Smith a bill of sale for him.

At Venture's behest, the two men met to determine which one would finally own him. Venture made no secret of his preference for Smith. It was finally agreed that Smith would settle accounts with Stanton and that Venture would move in with him.

Venture's instincts were good. Miner had used him as a financial pawn—a commodity speculation—and was evidently desperate to liquidate. He eventually ended up in debtor's prison.[46]

Oliver Smith Jr. was a physically big man like Venture and wore his authority and means without arrogance. A Groton native and a coastal and West Indies trader, he had married Stonington native Mary Denison in April 1759. In 1761, they moved to Mary's hometown and made plans to build a grand home, shop, and boat works on the Stonington waterfront. A strong, intelligent slave would clearly be an asset.

Although he owned slaves, Smith was not imbued with a rigid sense of entitlement or racial superiority. Local records suggest that he probably had firsthand knowledge of the emerging practice of manumission and questioned the morality of slavery. Richard Smith, another resident of Groton in 1757, who may or may not have been related, had freed a slave girl inherited by his wife. A Quaker, Richard spoke eloquently at the annual South Kingston Quaker Meeting, words that have been preserved in the Rhode Island Quaker records, about the evils of slavery and why he felt morally compelled to free the girl on her 18th birthday, the earliest that law allowed manumission: "the Lord by his free Goodness hath given me a clear sight of the cruelty of making a slave of one that was by nature as free as my own children."[47] This is one of the earliest examples of morally inspired emancipation in New England, an act that most likely did not escape the attention of Oliver Smith.

These events do not suggest that Venture's owner was especially compelled by the Christian church in his attitude toward slavery. If anything, he was more likely inspired by membership in the Freemasons, as was his mentor, George Washington. The Masonic Order followed a belief in a supreme being but primarily anchored itself to earthly concerns. Many Masons were leading businessmen in the community, and the Connecticut coast had become a center of the fraternal order in those days.

The average slave owner in the mid-18th century discouraged his slaves from converting to Christianity because it forced him to directly confront a moral problem: If a slave could be baptized, that meant he or she was truly a child of God and thus equal to any person in God's eyes.

Church-going was not encouraged for practical reasons, as well. For slaves, Sunday was the one day that belonged to them. It was their chance not only to be with family but also to work for themselves. Work on Sunday began before dawn and continued well into the night. Venture took full advantage of "his own day" during 25 years of enslavement, building the capital he would need to buy freedom for himself and his family.

Venture's new owner had consented to letting him purchase his freedom some day. This was a case of mutual benefit. To that end, Venture unearthed what was left of his savings and turned it over to Smith as a first installment. The year was 1761. *"This was the third time of my being sold, and I was then thirty-one years old."*

Venture had endured the crucible of chattel bondage in obscurity for two decades. Whether he knew it or not, he was about to pursue a course that would make him a legend in his own lifetime.

"Freedom's a matter of making history,
of venturing forth toward a time when freedom is free."

– MARILYN NELSON, *The Freedom Business*, 2005

THE TRANSITIONAL YEARS

Venture was determined to buy himself.

The 1760s were a time of growing political unrest in the American colonies. The French and Indian wars, which were really a struggle between European powers for expanded territory, finally ended after 13 years in 1763.

Although Britain would acquire Canada from the French and most of the North American colonies east of the Mississippi, the wars had taken a heavy toll on the British treasury, as well as blood. The colonies were starting to bear the financial brunt and they did not like it.

Taxes would become a major source of anger, but the British were also levying taxes on West Indian sugar and molasses. Northern ship captains and merchants resisted, declaring those products essential for the slave trade, a "vital commerce" for New England.[48]

Venture had his own money problems. Through the calumny of others, he lost a small fortune, more than a quarter of the amount he needed to buy his freedom. He had turned over his remaining savings to his new owner and was left with nothing. He had to start from scratch.

When a slave and owner agreed on a course of "redemption," it was necessary to enlist a middleman to administer the arrangement. Usually this was a professional person, like a judge, justice of the peace, or elected official. This person would hold the contract and the money that the slave paid toward his freedom. The agent kept the interest earned on the money as compensation. Only a free man could own property and therefore make a legal and binding contract. As Venture explained, *"I was the property of my master, and therefore could not safely take his obligation myself."* Property cannot own property. Venture turned to a friend, whom he only identified as a "free negro." This person was probably Primas Sikes, a longtime companion whose name crops up in several business transactions with Venture.[49] Although free, Sikes lived in the Thomas Stanton household at the time. As a go-between, his job would have been to take the owner's note of security and make the payments with money Venture gave him.

To make those payments Venture needed to earn money on the side. Smith had bought a slave and thus required his services. But when Venture was not needed in the Smith household, he worked on his own, primarily by fishing off Long Point and selling his catch in the Stonington market. He also sold vegetables he grew on a plot of land outside of town adjoining the Stanton farms.

"By cultivating this land with the greatest diligence and economy, at times when my master did not require my labor, in two years I laid up ten pounds." He turned over these precious proceeds, equal to about one-eighth of the agreed purchase price, to his friend to give to Smith.

Flush with success, Venture then prevailed on Smith to let him work for a full winter on his own to earn more money. Smith agreed on the condition that Venture turn over a quarter of his earnings. In effect, Venture would pay for the privilege of working for himself.

To Oliver Smith this was perfectly logical and fair. After all, a slave, by definition, was meant to serve at the pleasure and profit of his master. For Smith it was good business to contract out Venture in the winter when he did not need his labor.

What Venture's owner may have not known was that such an arrangement had its roots in Africa, specifically from the slave society in that part of Africa Venture came from. The process was called *murgu*, payment by slaves to their masters for the right to work on their own account.[50]

Smith, who counted George Washington among his friends and

would later earn colonel's rank in the Continental Army, had built with Venture's help a small empire that included merchant ships, a store, and a new home. He could afford now to give his trusted slave, who was 11 years his senior, more latitude.

From his first winter of chopping wood and fishing from the islands, Venture earned four pounds 16 shillings; 25 percent went to his owner as a fee and the remainder went toward paying off his purchase price.

And so it went, season by season, pound by pound, shilling by shilling.

Venture hired himself out to other men, once on Fishers Island and once for an autumn and winter on Long Island. During that later six-month period, he *"cut and corded four hundred cords of wood, besides threshing out seventy-five bushels of grain."*

It was a lean and Spartan existence. He allowed himself only

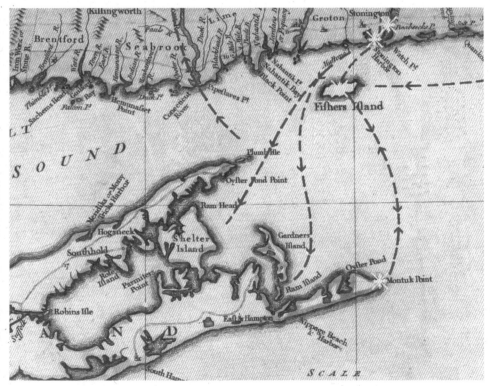

Map detail of eastern Long Island showing Ram Island, Shelter Island, and Montauk Point

one pair of new shoes, and the rest of his wages he tucked away. *"At night I lay on the hearth, with one coverlet over and another under me,"* he said.

In the spring of 1765, Venture returned to Stonington and paid Smith an installment that left nearly 14 pounds remaining on his debt. Smith, clearly awed by the man's determination, said that was enough. Venture could pay the rest later.

Venture had turned over 71 pounds, 2 shillings to his owner over a period of four years. That was an enormous sum in those days, enough to buy hundreds of acres of land. When Venture had asked Smith why he required such an *"unreasonable price,"* his owner said it was for future security in case Venture should become unable to work in his old age and should need to be supported. As mentioned previously, this was the law of the land to protect the Crown from having to support abandoned or infirm former slaves. But, after five years with his slave, Smith must have realized that Venture was unlikely to ever become a burden. This realization probably influenced his decision to waive the final payment.

Despite his complaint about the price, the transaction bought something that Venture would later call *"a privilege which nothing else can equal"* — his freedom.

Now in his late 30s, Venture breathed the air of liberty for the first time since he was a boy in Africa. He recalled the moment not as one of triumph, but as one of adversity surmounted:

> *I had already been sold three different times, made considerable money with seemingly nothing to derive it from, been cheated out of a large sum of money, lost much by misfortunes, and paid an enormous sum for my freedom.*

For one who had dreamed so long and worked so hard for his independence, this would seem to be an occasion for great celebration. There is no evidence of it. There are several possibilities for why that was. For one thing, Venture was not really the celebrating type. He was a very serious man. For another, he had good reason for bitterness. He might have become a free man much earlier if fate had been kinder.

Not least of all the reasons for somberness was the environment Venture was entering as a free man. Connecticut, and specifically New London County, had the largest concentration of slaves in New England at this time and one of the largest populations of free blacks.

Discrimination against free blacks was rampant. Nearby New London, for example, had a law on its books that forbade free blacks from living in the town, owning land, or going into business without the consent of town government.[51]

Technically free he may have been, but Venture knew that there were lesser degrees of freedom for a black man, even one of royal lineage.

The irony of the political struggle underway in the American colonies could not have escaped him. Whites were chafing at the bit of tyranny in 1765, but they treated it as an affront to them alone.

In March of that year, the British Parliament passed the Stamp Act, which imposed a tax on all newspapers, legal documents, playing cards, dice, almanacs, and pamphlets in the colonies—all precious commodities. The public was outraged, accusing Britain of imposing taxation without representation.

When Patrick Henry was accused of treason for opposing the tax, he replied: "If this be treason, make the most of it." Such boldness elevated him to the highest rank of patriotism. If a black had uttered such words, the reward would have been 40 lashes or worse.

No, if a black man were to succeed in such a world, it would have to be on the white man's terms. So be it. Venture would outdo the white man at his own game.

First, he would have to attend to certain practicalities. As a free man who would be entering into contractual agreements, Venture would need a full, legal name. He took the surname of Smith, his last owner.

The decision seemed in keeping with Venture's character and sense of priorities. He was a practical man, and Smith was not only a practical name in common use then, as today, but a highly influential one in the region. Oliver Smith was related by blood or marriage to the elite business class of Stonington and Groton. Unlike a later generation caught up in revolutionary fervor, Venture was uninterested in reinventing his identity or making any political statement. Slaves who earned their freedom fighting in the Continental Army after 1775 often took names that obliterated both their slave and African past.[52]

Venture was building on his past, not erasing it.

Dubious distinction though it may have been, Venture was owned by the right people. The Mumfords, Stantons, Miners, and Smiths constituted some of the leading families in southern New England. For example, a Mumford served as no less than Benjamin Franklin's personal secretary in Paris, circa 1783–1785. Stantons are listed on the monument to the Battle of Groton Heights, the 135-foot-tall obelisk that is the first Revolutionary War monument of its kind in the country erected to the fallen patriots. The list goes on.

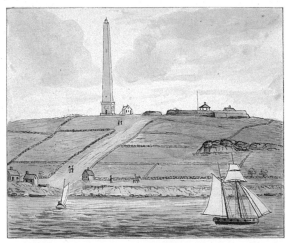

Memorial to the 1781 battle of Groton Heights
drawing by J. W. Barber

Perhaps most importantly, the name Smith belonged to Venture's only owner who kept his word.

Then there was the question of where to best earn a living. He wanted to be near his wife and three children, who were still in bondage to the Stantons. But work opportunities were limited in southeastern Connecticut, where most of the forestland had long ago been cleared and where an inordinately large population of blacks, free and slave, were already toiling.

Fate helped make the decision for him. A fire broke out at his lodging. Evidently an accident, it burned up a chest containing his clothes and 38 pounds in paper currency. Thoroughly discouraged, Venture sold what remaining possessions he had and moved to less-populated Long Island where landowners were in need of good workers.

More than 10 percent of the population of eastern Long Island was now black, and a large community of freed slaves had settled on Shelter Island in the fork of the larger land mass. Records of the time showed that shortly before the Revolution the population of blacks there was nearly 20 percent.[53] If Venture had joined up with them at any point, it is not mentioned in the Narrative, but given his strong independent streak, it is not likely he would have stayed for long.

It is important to note here that the toll of slavery at that time usually meant that a black man reached the end of his most productive life by his mid-30s, the age at which Venture was just setting out on his own.

Certainly his enormous size and stamina were central to his destiny. In the mid-1700s, the average man was about five feet six inches tall.[54] One who stood a head taller and carried a nine-pound ax like it was a fly swatter had no trouble finding work.

Venture spent his first four years on Long Island doing different kinds of work. This most notably included cutting "*several thousand*" cords of wood, which earned him the considerable sum of 207 pounds 10 shillings. According to economic historians, this sum was equal at the time to 14–17 years of wages for an average unskilled laborer.

Even the casual reader of Smith's narrative might wonder how someone could recall with such precision, some three decades after the fact, how much his labors earned and how much he paid out through his lifetime. The short explanation for this is that money was the way Venture kept score.

Although he berated himself for not having the education that allowed him to manage money well, he had a good head for figures. Perhaps it was inherited.

On the whole question of Venture's self-deprecating comment that he could not read or properly calculate figures, the evidence suggests that he knew enough to handle a basic contract, as well as to add and subtract. Given his proclivity for recalling in excruciating detail every transaction he ever made, his remark in the Narrative about people "*taking advantage of my ignorance of numbers*" smacks of disingenuousness. As any businessman knows, understating one's abilities can be a useful strategy.

Venture came from a culture of commerce. Like his father, who gave up his life to not surrender his wealth, Venture placed ultimate importance on amassing capital. But, as events would later demonstrate, he was not a miser who worshipped money for its own sake. He would spend freely to get what he wanted. For himself, however, he had few wants. As he noted in his Narrative:

> *Perhaps some may enquire what maintained me all the time I was laying up money. I would inform them that I bought nothing which I did not absolutely want. All fine clothes I despised in comparison with my interest, and never kept but just what clothes were comfortable for common days, and perhaps I would have a garment or two which I did not have on at all times, but as for superfluous finery I never thought it to be compared with a decent homespun dress, a good supply of money and prudence. Expensive gatherings of my mates I commonly shunned, and all kinds of luxuries I was perfectly a stranger to . . .*

And, he hastened to add, "*I never was at the expence of six-pence worth of spirits.*" His not being a drinker set him far apart from most of his contemporaries. Hard cider, beer, and liquor, especially rum, were not only plentiful and cheap but a great source of solace for both the oppressed and profligate (and a reliable source of potable liquid at a time when clean water was in short supply). In short, alcoholism was a major problem in 18th-century America.[55]

Venture's first big expense as a free man was the purchase of his two sons, Solomon and Cuff. While working on Ram Island, in the eastern end of Long Island, he bought them in 1769 for 200 dollars each, which amounted to two-thirds of his savings.

The decision to purchase his sons, who were then 14 and 12, before liberating his wife and daughter was a practical one. The boys carried with them potentially higher earning power. Whether white or black, a man's sons were his security for the future, and if they did not work for the home business, they were hired out.

The father and sons worked together for more than three years cutting wood, fishing, and farming wherever the opportunities arose around Long Island Sound and off the Rhode Island coast.

He then *"purchased a negro man"* who had asked Venture to take him, evidently so he could work for his own freedom some day. But instead, the slave ran away a short time later, leaving Venture 60 pounds in the lurch *"except twenty pounds which he paid me previous to his absconding."*

It was another broken trust. Venture had employed a customary African tradition to earn his own redemption and was clearly willing to give that opportunity to others of his race. But in the new world, his faith seemed destined to be betrayed.

If the reader is confused by the constantly changing currencies mentioned in the narrative, one might take solace in the fact that residents of the colonies at this time were almost equally confused. Everything from Spanish coins to English shillings and three kinds of paper currency were used in transactions, and some people carried around a conversion table to get them all straight. The basic currency of Connecticut in the 18th century was the British pound, but it was worth less than the pound sterling. At this particular time, a pound was worth about 2.66 in colonial dollars.[56]

After suffering this latest loss, Venture used his remaining money to buy land as an investment. Deed records indicate that in December 1770, after five years as a free man, he purchased 26 acres in Stonington next to his old nemesis, the Stanton family, who still owned his wife and daughter. This was not his first real-estate transaction. It is believed that when he was a slave, in about 1762, he used his free friend Sikes to buy six acres of land in Stonington for him. This was the same plot that Venture farmed to help earn his freedom.

A TABLE of the Value and Weight of COINS, as they now pass in England, Pennsylvania, and New-York.		Sterling.			Philad.			N. York			Weight.		Most Sorts of Spanish Silver are sold in London by the Ounce, and often varies, but seldom or ever exceeds 5s. 5d. In Pennsylvania it sells for 8s. 6d. per Ounce.
		£	s.	d.	£	s.	d.	£	s.	d.	dwt.	gr.	
	ENgl. Guineas at	1	1	0	1	14	0	1	16	0	5	6	
	French Guineas	1	1	0	1	13	6	1	15	0	5	5	
	Moidores - - -	1	7	0	2	3	6	2	6	0	6	18	
	Johannes's - - -	3	12	6	6	0	0	6	6	0	18	8	
	Half Johannes's -	1	16	0	3	0	0	3	3	0	9	4	
	French milled Pistoles	0	16	6	1	6	6	1	8	0	4	4	
	Spanish Pistoles	0	16	6	1	7	0	1	9	0	4	6	
	Doubloons	3	6	0	5	8	0	5	16	0	17	0	
	English Crowns	0	5	0	0	7	6	0	8	0	19	0	
	French Silver Crowns	0	5	0	0	7	6	0	8	0	17	6	
	* Spanish Pieces of 8				0	7	6	0	8	0	17	6	
	English Six-pence	0	0	6	0	0	9	0	0	9			

In Boston and Connecticut Pieces of Eight pass for 6s. and Gold by Weight.

Currency table in 1771

As a new decade opened, the spark of war had been lit with the Boston Massacre on March 5, 1770. Did Venture hear about Crispus Attucks, the sailor and fugitive slave of African and Indian descent who became the first man to die for American freedom? Like Venture, Attucks was a giant of a man, six feet two inches tall. They chose different paths. Venture insulated himself within a world he was trying to shape for himself and his family. But he could not wholly escape.

Death of Crispus Attucks at the Boston Massacre, 5 March 1770 chromolitho by James Wells Champney

In 1773 Venture hired out his eldest son, Solomon, to Massachusetts merchant Charles Church *"for one year, on consideration of his giving him* (Solomon) *twelve pounds and an opportunity of acquiring some learning."*

Church, it turned out, had contracted to hire hands for a whaling voyage from Nantucket, and persuaded Solomon, who was then 17, to join up. In addition to his wages, Church promised Solomon *"a pair of silver buckles,"* an enticement that would be equivalent today to a $300 pair of custom Nike sneakers.[57]

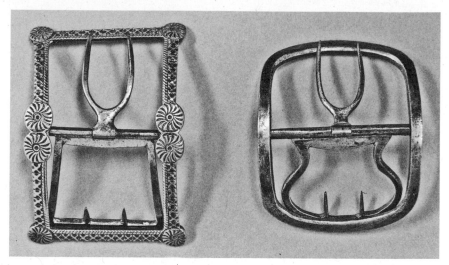

18th-century shoe buckles: at left, a fancy engraved silver dress buckle circa 1760–1770 and at right, a common steel buckle

When Venture heard about it, he rushed to the dock to try to prevent his son from leaving. The father knew the dangers one could encounter on such deep-sea voyages—having himself sailed for seven months on such a precarious mission—especially for an inexperienced youth. The lure of silver shoe buckles must have particularly rankled a man who had no tolerance for frivolities.

His eldest son, Venture had said, "*was all my hope and dependence for help.*" But he got there too late, with the vessel almost out of sight on the horizon. Venture's premonition proved true. Solomon died of scurvy on the voyage.

When recalling this tragedy, Venture said Church never paid him his son's wages. He also did not get the boy's share of the whale oil or the buckles. He added: "*In my son, besides the loss of his life, I lost equal to seventy-five pounds.*"

He was talking about what it had cost him to free Solomon four years earlier. While readers might find this a callous and unsentimental appraisal, Venture was expressing himself in the terms that he most valued. One could look more to action than to words when searching for clues to Venture Smith's humanity.

Now about 44 and flush from new profits made delivering wood by boat to the mainland, Venture negotiated with former owner

Thomas Stanton for the purchase of his wife, Meg. She cost him 40 pounds. The timing of this was partially motivated by economic savvy. Meg was seven months pregnant. If he had waited until the child was born, he would have had to buy two people.

Their third son was born in 1774, and they named him Solomon 2nd.

Venture also bought two more male slaves and let them both go. Finally, he purchased freedom for his oldest child, Hannah, who was then 21.

The year was now 1775, and the American colonies were embarking on a protracted war for independence. Venture's narrative amazingly makes no mention of this. He had just completed a remarkable quest for liberty on his own, and he summarized it succinctly:

> *I had already redeemed from slavery, myself, my wife and three children, besides three negro men.*

He had achieved political independence for his family, and now, on the eve of revolution around him, he embarked on the road of financial independence.

"He broke out of the system that enslaved him and triumphed over it."
— DAVID RICHARDSON, Wilberforce Institute, September 2005

THE FINAL YEARS

An interesting area of speculation is whether Venture ever met George Washington. It would initially seem unlikely because such an encounter was not mentioned in the Narrative, but neither was the entire Revolutionary War.

It is known that the commander of the Continental Army visited Oliver Smith in Stonington in April 1776 (the same year Smith named his tenth child George). Although Venture had already been a free man for a decade, he maintained close ties with the Smith family, and with the onset of war moved back to Connecticut in the winter of 1774–1775.

What makes the prospect of these two slave owners and a free black man standing in the same room together so enticing is their physical similarities. They all towered over their contemporaries. Gen. Washington was six feet two inches tall. Col. Smith was over six feet. Venture was six feet one and a half inches.[58]

Venture's size and prowess with an ax were so legendary that one modern historian could not resist the temptation to label him the "Black Paul Bunyan."[59] The moniker has been picked up by the mass media despite its historical irrelevance — Bunyan, of course, being a mythical giant created in the 19th-century upper Midwest.

It is noteworthy that most of the stories of Venture's physical prowess came from his later years. The reason is simple: Almost all the testimony to his feats came from witnesses who knew him during that later period in his life in the Connecticut interior. An 80-year-old man from the town of Moodus told a newspaper in 1894 that his father clearly remembered Venture being challenged while in his fifties by a noted wrestler in the area who "found he might as well try to remove a tree." Others talked of his ability to split seven cords of wood in a day.[60]

One can only imagine what the tales might have been like from those who knew Venture in his prime.

But in the area where he may have left his greatest mark, there is little mention — business. He was good at it.

Barely a decade out of enslavement, Venture Smith had already made a small fortune by growing and selling huge quantities of watermelons, net fishing and lobstering at night, and, for one seven-month stint on a whaler arranged by Smith in 1770, sharing in the profits from 400 barrels of oil. That was an enormous haul for a whaling voyage, and taking his share and some savings, Venture was able to purchase the 26 acres in Stonington. He bought it for 60 pounds and three years later sold it for 100 pounds.

Sloop *Union* of Boston, 1796, typical of sloops used in the triangular trade and for whaling

This was to become a pattern in his business success. Venture would take cash for his labor and, when possible, invest it in real estate that he would later sell at a significantly higher price.

"*My temporal affairs were in a pretty prosperous condition,*" he said of this period of his life. By 1774 he had already bought and sold a house and land in Stonington twice, owned a house and land on the far eastern end of Long Island, and had considerable cash savings.

This and my industry was what alone saved me from being expelled that part of the island in which I resided, as an act was passed by the select-men of the place, that all negroes residing there should be expelled.

This briefly mentioned incident not only reflects that Venture stood out among other men of his race but also alludes to a period of great turmoil as the northern colonies mobilized for war.

Sentiment for ending the institution of slavery was growing in the North, as the owner class throughout the colonies slaked its own thirst for political independence. John Jay of New York, who would later become the first chief justice of the U.S. Supreme Court, wrote: "It is much to be wished that slavery may be abolished . . . To contend for our own liberty, and to deny that blessing to others, involves an inconsistency not to be excused."

Many northern blacks were liberated and the newly freed became refugees. They set up camps outside settled townships, prompting expulsion edicts like the one Venture confronted on Long Island.

At the same time, there was a backlash among some slaveholders who tried desperately to protect their property by resurrecting moribund "slave codes" that greatly restricted those still in bondage.[61] Some owners handed over their slaves for safekeeping to friends in distant places in hopes of retrieving them when the conflict was over.[62]

On the eve of the Revolutionary War, the black population in North America numbered 567,000;[63] almost 90 percent were slaves on the plantations of the South. Although much smaller in numbers, blacks had become very much part of the northern fabric.

It was against this backdrop that Venture set a new course for himself and his family. Although an exception was made for him on Long Island, it was becoming clear that his kind were not welcome. He would go elsewhere.

But there was something else happening at about the time Venture decided to leave. It was called the War of Independence, and it was spreading south. British forces had their eyes on the abundant livestock throughout the Long Island basin.

Gen. Washington was well aware of the situation, and within four months after war ignited at Lexington and Concord, he issued a warning that the British were likely to raid the offshore islands "to plunder them and bring off what Cattle they may find." In a July 27, 1775, letter from Boston to the Continental Congress, he reported a "great Scarecity of fresh Provisions in the Enemy's Camp."

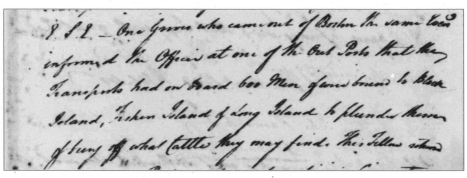

Detail of George Washington's letter to the Continental Congress in July 1775

He was right, but not soon enough. The British had already dispatched six ships from Boston that landed on Fishers Island on August 6, 1775, and plundered the livestock. Records show that they took "1,139 sheep, 3 milch Cows, one pair of Working Oxen, about 25 young Cattle, and ten Hogs,"[64] which they brought back through the blockade to the starving Tories and troops.

The patriots also played the game. In 1775 Thomas Mumford, a nephew of George Mumford, and New London merchant Na-

Article in the *New London Journal*, published August 11, 1775, about British supply raid.

thaniel Shaw loaded up a ship with cattle and sailed it to the West Indies, where they traded the beef for badly needed gunpowder.

After numerous British raids for supplies in the Long Island basin, Gen. Washington repeated his call for preventative action nearly a year later. In a letter to Gov. Jonathan Trumbull Sr. of Connecticut on July 9, 1776, he urged that the "great Quantities" of livestock and provisions on Fishers, Block, Plumb and Elizabeth islands, and on Martha's Vineyard "be removed quite out of the reach of the Enemy."[65]

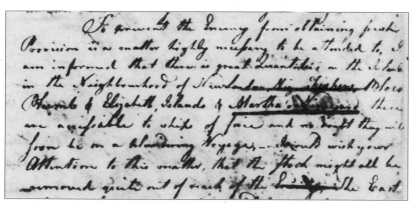

Detail of signed letter from George Washington to Gov. Trumbull of Connecticut in July 1776

The residents, however, remained slow to respond. The British launched aggressive forays, clashed with American militias, and finally captured the whole of Long Island and Manhattan in August 1776 and held them until the end of the war.

The British attached such importance to this area as a continuing source of provisions for the West Indian colonies, as well as for their troops, that the English Parliament passed a special law exonerating all Caribbean governors of treason for trading with the enemy.

As for Venture Smith, he was in his late forties, an age considered old for most mortals. He now had his entire family together, purchased by his own hand. After ten years of nonstop itinerant work, it was time for stability.

Venture had seen the war coming his way for some time. He and his family joined a mass evacuation of Long Island a good year before it became occupied by the British. Some slaves and free blacks linked up with the Tory exodus to New Brunswick and Nova Scotia. Venture chose the route of the Patriots across the sound to Connecticut.

But, always the consummate businessman, he managed to sell his property before the British seized it, and, with family in tow, arrived in a part of the world with which he had already become quite familiar.

When he got to Connecticut, Venture chose to settle in the

East Haddam on the Connecticut River drawing by J. W. Barber

lightly populated, but commercially active communities of Haddam and East Haddam, on the Connecticut River.

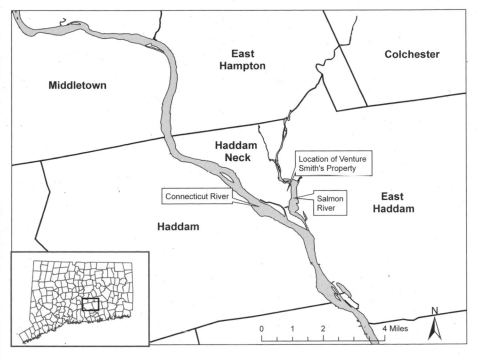

Location of Haddam Neck, where Venture built his farm and home

This may have seemed an odd settlement choice for a man whose experience in Connecticut had been exclusively along the southeastern coast. Haddam was 18 miles upriver and a long day's ride from the Stonington and New London areas. But Venture always kept his eyes and ears open for new opportunities, and this part of the Connecticut River south of Hartford, where the wider and deeper waters were ideal for boat traffic and trade, had already proved its mercantile worth.

An example of the kind of provisioning activity found in East Haddam at the time could be found in the cargo record of a ship bound for Grenada, a new British colony, in 1764. The ship carried an entire prefabricated house of white oak, two outbuildings, horses, oxen, sheep, geese, ducks, hay, and several carpenters with enough foodstuffs for them while they erected the house on the West Indian island.

He knew the key role this area played in the colonial economy. Next door in Salem was the enormous Browne plantation, owned by Col. William Browne of Massachusetts. As Browne was branded a Tory sympathizer, the Connecticut government confiscated his 9,536-acre plantation in 1779, thus taking possession of one of the most important northern provisioners of the West Indies. Coincidentally it had been managed by members of the prolific Mumford family, Browne's cousins. Col. Browne ended up governor of the British island of Bermuda.

From the outset, Venture knew what he wanted. He had his eye on a piece of high ground on Haddam Neck overlooking a cove on the Salmon River, a tributary of the Connecticut.

Mouth of the Salmon River by J. W. Barber; Venture's farm at Haddam Neck is on the ridge to the left of the sailboat in the center background

But instead of using his capital, Venture would work for it. He

> For the Confideration of *Twenty Pounds Lawful money*
> Received to *my*
> full Satisfaction, of *Venture a free negro Refident in Haddam*
> *in the County aforr* Do Give, Grant, Bargain, Sell and Confirm unto the faid
> *Venture & his heirs & affigns forever One Certain Tract of Land*
> *Lying in ad Haddam Bounded as follows (viz) Beginning at a Stake*

Detail of deed for Venture's first land purchase at Haddam Neck, March 3, 1775

hired himself out to others for about 11 weeks, and with the proceeds, on March 3, 1775, Venture purchased his first 10 acres from a local farmer, Abel Bingham. Venture summarized what happened next as if he were cutting butter with his ax:

> *On this land I labored with great diligence for two years, and shortly after purchased six acres more of land contiguous to my other. One year from that time I purchased seventy acres more of the same man, and paid for it mostly with the produce of my other land. Soon after I bought this last lot of land, I set up a comfortable dwelling house on my farm, and built it from the produce thereof.*

Not all was well, however. His eldest child, Hannah, had fallen

Boundaries of Venture's farm at Haddam Neck in March 1778, with overlays by Cameron Blevins

THE FINAL YEARS

into bad health. She was free now, and had married another free black by the name of Isaac, whom Venture called "*a dissolute and abandoned wretch*" who let her languish in her illness.

I therefore thought it best to bring her to my house and nurse her there. I procured her all the aid mortals could afford, but notwithstanding this she fell a prey to her disease, after a lingering and painful endurance of it.

In reporting his daughter's death, Venture could not help but mention that the attending doctor charged him 40 pounds. Again we see it: A gentle and grieving father who measured his loss in numbers.

Two years later, he faced another event that sheds more light on his nature and abilities.

In his mid-fifties, Venture hired two freed slaves to work for him. One, named Mingo, overspent his wages and borrowed eight dollars from Venture. He then ran away. Venture procured an arrest warrant from a local judge and tracked Mingo down. Mingo refused to accompany Venture to the judge's chambers, and the Narrative described what happened next:

I took him on my shoulders, and carried him there; distant about two miles. The justice asking me if I had my prisoner's note with me, and replying that I had not, he told me that I must return with him and get it. Accordingly I carried Mingo back on my shoulders, but before we arrived at my dwelling, he complained of being hurt, and asked me if this was not a hard way of treating our fellow creatures. I answered him that it would be hard thus to treat our honest fellow creatures. He then told me that if I would let him off my shoulders, he had a pair of silver shoe-buckles, one shirt and a pocket handkerchief, which he would turn out to me. I agreed, and let him return home with me on foot; but the very following night, he slipped from me, stole my horse and has never paid me even his note.

Time and time again Venture would give his trust, only to have it broken. This he could never abide, and he would demand justice.

But his kind heart would prevail again, and that too would be broken. It might seem strange that Venture did not talk about those trusts that were kept, although we know there were some. For example, two free black men, Whacket and Peter, bought land from Venture and conducted other transactions. They proved themselves to be honest men. But, for Venture, that was expected behavior and perhaps that is why he chose not to mention it.

We learn at the end of Venture's narrative that his two remaining sons also broke his heart, but we do not know how. He does not talk much about his relationship with them. It is important to note here that Venture dictated his narrative seven years before his death, so there is that unrecorded period during which he might have changed his mind. We do know from other testimony that his second living son, Solomon, cared for both parents in their final years and is buried with them.

It is known from records and oral histories that Cuff enlisted in the Continental Army in January 1781 for three years and fought against the British until the war ended late in 1783.

In the early days of the war, Congress had sought to remove blacks from the army, but later recanted because of the dire need for manpower and because the British forces were recruiting blacks with

Grave marker in Washington, Connecticut, for black revolutionary patriot Jeff Liberty, who served in an all-black regiment

the promise of freedom.[66] Connecticut was a leader in the campaign to recruit black soldiers for the colonial cause. In the end, some 5,000 men of African descent had joined the colonial forces, while some 800 had signed on with the British. The latter figure does not include the thousands who deserted from slavery to the British lines.[67]

Cuff had joined the regular army, one of an estimated 400-plus blacks in service from Connecticut, but he did not enlist in either of the colony's two all-black regiments. How much action he saw is not known. There was plenty going on at the time. In 1781 Benedict Arnold led a British force up the Connecticut River and burned to the ground New London and part of Groton. In the Battle of Groton Heights a slave by the name of Jordan Freeman fought alongside his owner and killed the British major leading the charge before he himself was slain. Freeman's owner, Col. William Ledyard, the commander of the patriot forces in the battle, died while surrendering.

Bronze plaque showing slave Jordan Freeman killing a British officer

The turncoat Benedict Arnold, himself from the New London area, used the occasion to settle some scores. He ordered his troops to torch certain houses, including that of Thomas Mumford, a wartime adviser to Gov. Trumbull and the man who helped procure the precious gunpowder for the cause early in the war.

Venture's reaction to all this is not recorded. The news could not have escaped him that the year after he returned to Connecticut the history-making Declaration of Independence was forged. But the document failed to resolve the conflict over the institution of slavery. He may not have known how extensively the slavery issue was debated before the compromise was made to appease the southern colonies, but it did not matter. What mattered to Venture Smith were results.

The hypocrisy of an oppressed colony going to war for freedom that it was denying to others was not lost on all in the white community either. In 1774, Abigail Adams wrote to her husband, John: "I wish most sincerely there was not a slave in the province — It always appeared a most iniquitous scheme to me — fight ourselves for what we are daily robbing and plundering from those who have as good a right to freedom as we have — you know my mind upon this subject."[68]

Abigail Adams

Excerpt from Abigail's 1774 letter to her husband John Adams

THE FINAL YEARS

Most blacks who joined up did so in exchange for their freedom, but Cuff was already a free man. Given Venture's skepticism and highly practical nature, he may not have approved of his oldest son's enlistment. But it would be unfair to assume that his heart did not speak in a conversation that fathers and sons have had since time began. The parting had to have been wrenching. But Cuff returned from the war apparently unscathed and joined his father and brother in the quest for civilian prosperity.

An interesting side note: Memorials to the Revolutionary War dead commonly listed them all, including African Americans, in alphabetical order, sometimes with the word "Negro" after the name. It appears that the only time men of color achieved equality was in death.

Detail of plaque honoring those killed, wounded, and captured in the battle of Groton in 1781, listing "negros" Jordan Freeman and Lambo Latham among others

In the 23 years between his arrival at Haddam Neck and telling his story to the schoolteacher Elisha Niles in 1798, Venture Smith had amassed more than 130 acres of land, *"three habitable dwelling houses,"* no fewer than 20 boats and canoes, and dry docks, barns, and warehouses. He was the equivalent of today's millionaire.

But as an old man, Venture's memory was plagued by disappointments. He dwelled toward the end of his story on incidents where he was *"cheated out of considerable money by people whom I traded with taking advantage of my ignorance of numbers."* He also related bitterly the humiliation of being forced in court in 1790 to pay damages for a lost hogshead of molasses that was not his fault.

He summarized his life as follows:

I am now sixty nine years old. Though once strait and tall, measuring without shoes six feet one inch and an half, and every way well proportioned, I am now bowed down with age and hardship. My strength which was once equal if not superior to any man whom I have ever seen, is now enfeebled so that life is a burden, and it is with fatigue that I can walk a couple of miles, stooping over my staff. Other griefs are still behind, on account of which some aged people, at least, will pity me. My eye-sight has gradually failed, till I am almost blind, and whenever I go abroad one of my grand-children must direct my way; besides for many years I have been much pained and troubled with an ulcer on one of my legs. But amidst all my griefs and pains, I have many consolations; Meg, the wife of my youth, whom I married for love, and bought with my money, is still alive. My freedom is a privilege which nothing else can equal.

What Venture Smith neglected to say in this conclusion is that through dint of hard work, legendary accomplishments, and unyielding adherence to his principles, he had earned unprecedented respect from a society acculturated against giving it.

By the end of his life, Venture Smith was the equal of any man in community status and was regarded by many as without peer. It was not in his nature to publicly concede that. But he knew it.

The five men who certified his narrative were leading citizens of New London County, including Col. Smith's son, Edward.

It is both intriguing and frustrating for historians that Venture's narrative makes no mention of his religious beliefs or origins. We do not know the religion or beliefs of his African family. Whatever they were, it would have been difficult for him, especially during his 15 years with the Mumfords on isolated Fishers Island, to practice the beliefs of his ancestors.

There is no evidence that Venture formally joined the Christian faith in his new homeland. Niles, the fervently Christian scribe who recorded Venture's story, would have certainly made mention of such a conversion or membership in any church. Because Venture was unable to read, he would not have been able to utilize the all-important Bible in observing the faith; although he could have memorized key passages from oral teachings, as so many did. Tantalizingly there are several Biblical references in Venture's Narrative[69] and on his tombstone is inscribed "sacred to . . . "

The evidence clearly suggests that this man was a believer, but a private one.

The family plot in East Haddam Cemetery, showing gravestones for, from left, Solomon, Eliza, Marget, and Venture

Venture Smith died on September 19, 1805. Meg outlived him by four years.

Venture and Meg are buried side by side in the cemetery of the First Congregational Church of East Haddam, which from 1792 to this day has been the final resting place of the white establishment in that community.

The church was built only 11 years before Venture died. Because he was such a successful member of the community by then, it is likely that Venture Smith was approached for a donation if not also solicited for membership. The head of the building committee was Epaproditus Champion, leading businessman of East Haddam who

Gen. Epaproditus Champion

had been crucial in the supply effort during the Revolution. He would later provide a pallbearer for Venture's funeral. What exactly the agreement was we may never know, but clearly this was the man who had the power and the respect for Venture to make available in a prime location in the new cemetery a family plot for this former slave.

To Venture, this may have been his most important real estate transaction.

Ninety years later, in a published retrospective about Venture Smith's life, an elderly Haddam resident, Robert Cone, said his father had told him about Venture's funeral where he had served as a pallbearer.

The heavy body of the deceased was conveyed in a boat across the cove and carried on a bier the distance of three miles to the cemetery.

The two pallbearers in front were white and the two in back were black slaves. From the weight, one of the slaves complained: "It makes the gravel stones crack under my feet."

Venture was laid to rest under a brown tombstone carved by John Isham, with a winged cherub's head at the crest. This angel of immortality is graced with an African nose, Isham's way of showing respect for Venture and honoring his origins. The inscription, still clearly legible in the stone, reads:

Sacred to the Memory
of Venture Smith an
African tho the son of a
King he was kidnapped
& sold as a slave but by
his industry he acquired
Money to purchase his
Freedom who Died Sep 19th
1805 in y 77 Year of his
Age

Sacred to the Memory of Venture Smith an African, tho the son of a King he was kidnapped & sold as a slave but by his industry he acquired Money to purchase his Freedom who Died Sep 19th 1805 in ye 77th Year of his Age

My freedom is a privilege which nothing else can equal ...
It gives me joy to think that I have and that I deserve so good
a character, especially for truth and integrity.

—VENTURE SMITH, 1798

CONCLUSION

What made Venture Smith so special? He was, after all, only one of nearly half a million Africans forcibly brought to these shores. Other slaves had told their stories for posterity. Others had earned their freedom long before it became the law of the land. And others left a lineage of descendants.

Historians say Venture Smith put a rare human face on an anonymous, oppressive, and unconscionably long institution in America. They also say he contibuted greatly to the knowledge of an American slave's African origins and capture. And they say he provided an invaluable glimpse into the specific practice of northern slavery, a reality that had largely been suppressed in the flush of victory in the Civil War.

All this is true, but there is more to it than that. What makes Venture Smith special is the man himself and what he was able to accomplish by dint of his own perseverance, abilities, and opportunities.

It is too easy to attribute Venture's success to just "hard work." His dominant physical presence, extraordinary constitution, good health, brains, savvy, Africa-rooted sense of honor, and unwavering determination all contributed to the process. Venture never gave up, despite all his setbacks.

By the time Venture Smith died on September 19, 1805, he had become a fully vested and respected American. It was an earned status, not a conferred one. Venture succeeded in a world in which he was not meant to succeed. How he accomplished that is what makes his story so exceptional.

In a sense Venture lived the American dream. But what a gentle phrase for such an arduous journey. Unlike so many immigrants to these shores, he began his journey as another man's property and not as a recognized member of the society he entered. Yet he overcame that overwhelming obstacle and became a property owner himself.

Although the core of his narrative suggests that "property" was important to him, the deeper evidence shows that a sense of "*truth and integrity*" – qualities he never abandoned – defined his essence.

There are many mysteries about Venture Smith left unsolved, and one must admit that they have inspired continuing curiosity to this day about the man and his times. But he was not one to be coy – dangling tantalizing clues that would keep his name alive.

What was omitted in his narrative about his life – a time when even those who were experiencing these tumultuous years realized it was a crucial period in American history – may have been the work of his biographers but was, more likely, his own intention.

Venture's failure to mention the American Revolution, or the Declaration of Independence that served as the new country's philosophical foundation, or even his son Cuff having served in that conflict may have been his way of expressing his disappointment. These were events that to him constituted a betrayal of his trust. To him, they were broken promises.

We hold these truths to be self-evident, that all men are created equal;

He knew that "all men are created equal" did not apply to him. He would have to make it so. And he did. By the 1790s Venture and the new nation had both succeeded, and despite his earlier skepticism, the nation had kept its promise to him. Although slavery would remain a stain on America for another seven decades, Venture could not have accomplished what he did if the political climate had disallowed it.

He may have once believed in the Revolution and the American dream – he certainly joined with the Patriots in fleeing Long Island to Connecticut in 1775 – but toward the end of his life when he told his story, there was no evidence of it. He did not talk of the failed promise of achieving equality. Rather, when people disappointed him, he let examples of their broken word and trust speak for themselves. He died less than 18 months before Congress outlawed the Atlantic slave trade, and it would be another 60 years before Lincoln and the Civil War freed the enslaved people.

Venture's narrative ends on a negative note. Clearly he was tired of life, a crippled, semi-blind, and embittered man when he told his life story to Elisha Niles. For the first time in his life, he had to depend on others. He was a man who had lived his whole life on his own – dependent on no one but his beloved wife, Meg. The young took care of and venerated the old in those days, but there was little sign in the Narrative that his own children did so. Because Venture was a lifelong loner, he perhaps brought this on himself and it may be one reason why he showed so little sentimentality or closeness to others.

He judged himself, his children, the people he did business with, and his adopted country against a standard impossible to achieve – the image of his father that he had created from a child's memories. To Venture, his father was perfection. The son remembered him as "*a man of remarkable strength and resolution, affable, kind and gentle, ruling with equity and moderation.*"

For reasons he did not explain, Venture was disappointed by his children. Clearly they did not, nor could they have ever lived up to the standards by which he judged them – the standards he applied to his father and himself. He lived his life working dawn to dusk seven days a week to create a better life for his wife and children, and yet, like many first-generation immigrants, he was resentful when his children enjoyed the life of privileged offspring of a wealthy and successful peer of the community.

We can only speculate about what in his children disappointed him. In the summer of 1783, like many enlisted soldiers, did Cuff sell his pay voucher or bounty land, awarded to him for military service, for a little cash while waiting to be deactivated and allowed to return home? If so, Venture would have been appalled.

On the other hand, in 1802, land records show that Solomon paid off his father's mortgage on the farm. His sons kept Venture's legacy alive. But when the family re-published his narrative in 1835 the following closing section was omitted: "*O! that they had walked in the way of their father. But a father's lips are closed in silence and in grief! – Vanity of vanities, all is vanity!*"

The unanswered questions of religion and its absence from Venture's narrative we have largely attributed to the man's private and pragmatic character. Sunday may have been the Sabbath and thus a day of rest for the white establishment believers, but for Venture it was another day to work. Indeed, it would have been his principal day of personal work until he gained his freedom. He would have regarded all that time in church as time wasted.

Interestingly, some slave owners regarded religious practice as dangerous, for baptizing made all men equal in the eyes of God. These same owners were happy to give their slaves a day off if it was better spent tending their own gardens, fishing, or selling products of their labor to earn some personal money, rather than spent mulling over uncomfortable moral questions or dwelling on their woes through hymns.

There are no indications that Venture's owners took a position on religion, but, given Venture's strong independent streak, it is unlikely he would have been swayed on the question.

Venture never mentioned the religion practiced by his African family. During the 18th century, the two dominant religions in West Africa were the traditional, which Europeans called "animism" after the Latin word for "soul," and Islam, which had gradually been introduced by Arab traders and adopted by some ethnic groups. The two belief systems co-existed and intermingled throughout the region, with a common tenet that the spiritual and temporal worlds are unified.

Stripping the identity of the victims of the Middle Passage was one of the cruelest acts of the slave trade. Knowing who we are and where we come from are basic issues for all people. Beating slavery, gaining economic freedom, and retaining his identity were Venture's three great struggles. Venture knew who he was and struggled his entire life to retain his African and American identities.

In his final act in the East Haddam cemetery, this illiterate man did what none of his educated former owners managed to do. He left an identity and a legacy that would survive him through the ages. The Smith family plot, in a cemetery adjacent to one of the most important churches in Connecticut, is an anomaly. Unlike almost everyone else buried there, Venture did not belong to the church. Even today people belong to the church just so they can be buried in historic East Haddam Cemetery.

Venture saw himself as an American and a respectable middle-class one at that. He was underlining his freedom in terms his contemporary associates would recognize. As with his narrative, his burial and gravestone are statements about his freedom as an African-born American. For many 18th-century abolitionists, freedom was identified with religion, and Venture's burial in a place of significance in East Haddam Cemetery underlines how much he had internalized this philosophy and that he recognized some ultimate higher being. The burial site and Venture's final epitaph "*sacred to . . .*" punctuate this.

Venture was unusual in his capacity to rebuild a new life, to reinvent himself in a new world focused on the future while not forgetting where he came from. His own narrative and words on his tombstone were a way of confirming his acceptance of the written word as a substitute for the oral traditions of his African heritage. Yet he never compromised his basic principles, learned from his father: Truth, honesty, and his word.

Venture was permanently reaffirming who he was, where he came from, and what he accomplished – his final statement carved in stone. Venture commissioned an American masterpiece to make this statement – an extraordinary tombstone, a major work of folk art created by sculptor and carver John Isham.

It is fitting that the work of art protecting Venture's legacy was the product of another man's hard work. Venture's size and strength had made him ideal as a builder of post-and-beam buildings and probably constituted a major reason why both Thomas Stanton and then Oliver Smith bought him. Most important, these qualities helped Venture earn his freedom.

In 1765, after gaining his freedom, Venture was able to put race and his own experiences of enslavement aside to build a future and legacy for his family. He truly began from scratch, for unlike most immigrants, he started with absolutely no capital. He also began with no family or other support group. But he managed to acquire an understanding of American shipping, trading, and business practices from observing his owners (particularly the Mumfords and Smiths), and, after freeing himself from the bonds of slavery, succeeded in achieving the American dream.

Venture, who came to this country as a traded commodity, another man's property and investment, achieved success by becoming a trader in commodities with the very people and system that had subjugated him.

Recently Archbishop Desmond Tutu, head of the Truth and Reconciliation Commission in South Africa, spoke at the Wilberforce Institute for the study of Slavery and Emancipation on the 200th bicentenary of the end of the British Slave Trade. He addressed the need for the victims and the perpetrators of crimes against humanity to heal. He emphasized that victims must put hatred and a desire for retaliation behind them and join with the perpetrators, working together to build a common future. Venture Smith accomplished this enlightened relationship with Oliver Smith, the Mumfords, and then their offspring. All put slavery behind them and joined together for 40 years as successful businessmen and neighbors – truly one of the great lessons Venture taught us.

One cannot leave this story without harking back to the striking

Col. Oliver Smith Jr. House built in 1761, Stonington, Connecticut

name of our subject. Shakespeare noted that a rose would "smell as sweet" by any other name. What about "Venture"? The name is clearly a caricature, bestowed insensitively by a white man who viewed another human being as a property investment. Mockingly contrived as labels rather than identities, such names were commonly imposed on slaves to relegate them to the status of lesser beings. So why did Venture choose to retain this name after gaining his independence and not select one of greater dignity?

First, he was not ashamed of his name. If he ever had doubts, perhaps provoked by the snickering of strangers, it was his nature not to succumb. He would wear his name as a badge of honor.

Further, beyond any question of pride, the concept of "venture" became his true identity. It is a name he grew into, and he shaped his life by it. It is not an exaggeration to say he was a venture capitalist before the phrase became part of America's lexicon: He invested in himself; he invested in the earth and its productive power, in real estate, in shelter, and in many other utilitarian things. He also invested in his sons and in his African-American brethren, although these were investments that often disappointed him.

Venture made the name fit him. No greater testimony to that can be found than what is carved in the stone of his grave marker: "Venture Smith an African."

We know of no other survivor of the Middle Passage to North America in the 17th or 18th century who has left us so much.

We began his story by exclaiming: "If only Venture Smith could write," we would have had a greater legacy. But, in fact, he left us with more than most.

———

"He is richest whose honor outlives him."

–MARILYN NELSON, Connecticut Poet Laureate, 2005

"This extraordinary problem which sooner or later the entire world has to face up to, is how people of very different ethnic backgrounds can learn to live together on this earth."
—PETE SEEGER, March 2001

EPILOGUE

When contemplating Venture's legacy, many questions come to mind. How many people in the world know who he was and where he came from? Do people still look up to him? Does his family still exist?

Venture lives on foremost in his family, some of whom still reside just a few miles from his farm some 200 years later. To date, genealogists have documented more than 9,000 descendants of Venture and Meg, spanning 11 generations. It is not known exactly how many are alive, but family members as far away as California are stepping forward.

One has only to visit the cemetery in East Haddam on any September 19th, the anniversary of Venture's death, to see his descendants and others from the area gathered together to honor Venture and Meg.

However, the Documenting Venture Smith Project, initially inspired by the family, is spreading Venture's legacy to a wider world. This project has been described by scholars as the largest research enterprise ever mobilized to trace a survivor of the Middle Passage from his birth in Africa to enslavement and on to freedom in America.

Venture's magnificent tombstone, his remarkable narrative, and the legendary stories about him added further inspiration and motivation to this effort. But, beyond that, what has struck this unusual coalition of scholars, scientists, poets, archaeologists, historians, and civil rights activists is the story of a slave who reinvented himself.

Venture decided that he and his family would become free, be successful—economically, socially, and politically—and become fully
vested Americans. To do this he had to set aside past persecution, injustice, and inequality to work with the very people who had owned
and mistreated him.

As his story unfolded, it became clear that Venture was as much
a founder of this country as were his owners—the Smiths, the Stantons, and the Mumfords—many of whose descendants also still live in
Connecticut. On July 4, 1776, whether he knew or not, Venture embarked on a journey to build a new country with no less a role than
that of the founding fathers. Although the full promise of equality
and freedom for him and other African Americans had not yet been
achieved, the new country delivered an unprecedented opportunity.

Among the tangible legacies left to us by Venture's story are the
numerous physical sites that still exist today. These include:

The slave castles on the Gold Coast, in present-day Ghana. Although
the specific castle where young Broteer was held is not known, the
major fortresses of that period have been restored and can be seen
today.

The homes of his owners. Robert Stanton's Stonington house is
largely untouched since Venture's time, even down to much of
the original furniture. The foundation and site of Thomas Stanton's house is in a state sanctuary area,[70] and Oliver Smith's
house, which Venture helped build, can also still be seen today in
Stonington.

Venture's first farm. The land Venture farmed and the foundation
of his first house are located in the same state sanctuary.

Venture's farm in Haddam Neck. The home and farm that Venture
built for his family after they were freed is a pristine archaeological
site, ironically because a nuclear power plant was built there in the
20th century. The owner, Connecticut Yankee Atomic Power, has
recognized the importance of Venture's farm site and its place in
American history. The corporation, which decommissioned the
plant in 2006, has strived to preserve the site and has financed years

of intensive digging and documentation under the leadership of archaeologists Lucianne Lavin and Mark Banks.

The family's burial site in East Haddam Cemetery. The excavations and gravestone carvings have provided a wealth of information that has only begun to be interpreted. The Wilberforce Institute and the Beecher House Center are working to have both the family farm and the East Haddam gravesite formally recognized by UNESCO and linked to its World Heritage Site in Anomabu.

Robert Stanton House in Stonington, 300 years later

Then there is the science. Archeology and modern genetics research are helping us learn more about the origins of people like Venture and Meg. For example, we do not know the exact location of Venture's birth or anything about Meg's origins, not even her country of origin. DNA tracking may help provide answers.

At the family's request, the Documenting Venture Smith Project opened the East Haddam graves in July 2006, a project supervised by Connecticut State Archaeologist Nicholas Bellantoni. Samples recovered from Meg's grave were taken to the University of Connecticut's new Center of Applied Genetics and Technology where scientists continue their investigation. In addition, DNA research on the Smiths' living descendants is also being conducted. Thanks to comprehensive genealogical records researched by the family and Dr. Karl P. Stofko, historian of the East Haddam Church, the Project is mapping the full genetic landscape of Venture, his family, and his descendants.

View of East Haddam cemetery and church during 2006 excavation project

In explaining some of the DNA conclusions, the center's director, Dr. Linda Strausbaugh, reported in September 2006: "From the family tree of Meg and Venture's descendants, we can infer back to one 5th generation female founder who has a mitochondrial type that moved in early human history out of the Near East to explore surrounding areas. It is, interestingly, not typically associated with the main African types, but is currently found in a wide distribution,

Excavation project
leaders: Chandler Saint
and Nicholas Bellantoni

including Europe, northern Africa, India, Arabia, northern Caucasus
Mountains, and the Near East. In addition to this lineage, Venture
and Meg's family includes other genetic components from across the
world, including six different African types that represent each of the
major human lineages within the continent, as well as the major
European mitochondrial type. These results represent only a frac-
tion of the family tree and we expect that as additional family members are identified and better databases become available, future
research will reveal Venture's genetic legacy to be even more diverse."

But like history, science cannot tell us everything. We may never
know, for example, exactly where Venture was born in the interior of
the Gold Coast. Despite extensive research by contemporary scholars, entire places, people and even languages were evidently wiped
out in the fight over territory, resources and slave populations during the 18th century and later. No map or written record of Venture's
homeland, Dukandarra, survived, except for the description in his

The excavation work at the Venture Smith Family gravesite in East Haddam on August 2, 2006

narrative. Scholars now believe that Venture's people are a "lost tribe."

The assumption that DNA alone can give instant answers, as purveyed in television programs and the mass media, is a fiction, but science can help confirm or deny genealogical records. The family tree loses much of its accuracy as one traces along each branch — often because the listed father of a child is not always the real father.

We talked previously about Venture being owned by the "right" people. Every American success story requires something that one might call chance, luck, or opportunity. The individual must recognize it, seize it, and then utilize his own assets (brains, physical strength, energy, and determination) to capitalize on the opportunity. Venture took advantage of the social capital he accumulated while living as a captive on Fishers Island with the Mumfords to start reinventing himself and ultimately freeing himself and his family. He looked to the future, not the past, and changed his status from a piece of property to a working businessman and finally to a builder of part-nerships that cemented his and his family's future.

Earlier we asked if people will remember Venture Smith and if people still look up to him. The enthusiasm generated by Venture's story on the 200th anniversary of his death in 2005 can only elicit a resounding *yes!*

Although up to this point the Documenting Venture Smith Project has focused on historical documentation of the facts of Venture's life and will continue working to discover new information and refine what we know, from now on the focus will be on public awareness and effecting social change. We expect that Venture's story will have a broader influence—an influence that will help us stimulate popular interest in the history of slavery in the Atlantic, the Caribbean, New England, and the Long Island basin.

We anticipate that new information uncovered in historical soci-eties, libraries, town records, and attics—information previously ignored because its significance was unrecognized—will increase our understanding of Venture's story. Most importantly, the Project will use Venture's experience to explain contemporary slavery and work to eradicate it.

So Venture's story lives on, and this book is not the beginning of the end. Rather it might well be called the end of the beginning.

————

"I'd like to see Venture in the history books, but in the *school* history books. I think slavery is a very painful subject for America and we need to start healing, and perhaps Venture can be one of those vehicles to help in the healing process."

−Florence P. Warmsley, 8th-generation descendant of Venture Smith

The following is a facsimile of Venture Smith's original Narrative, printed by *The Bee* in New London, CT, December 1798, 32 pages (originally with a plain blue cover). This is the first time it has been republished in its original form. Page 32 is a certificate attesting to the veracity of the Narrative by five leading citizens of Stonington, CT, dated November 3, 1798. Pages 4-32 are from the copy in the Connecticut Historical Society and are full size, while the title page, often improperly referred to as "the cover," is 75%. The title page and its reverse are from the Beinecke Rare Book and Manuscript Library Yale University copy. This one is particularly interesting because it appears to have been Venture's or his family's own copy. Handwritten corrections to the spelling of several of the African names are on the cover; and on page 32, the name "Venture Smith" is written in the location where owners often put their names.

Readers unfamiliar with pre-19th-century printed text may be confused by some of the type characters, especially the use of the "long s". The "long s", which looks almost like an "f" was a holdover from earlier manuscript writing. In Venture's Narrative we find both the "long s" and the "normal s". The "normal s" is used at the end of words, and also when it is capitalized. In other places, the "long s" (which resembles an "f") is used. Example: The modern form of "seamstress" becomes "feamftrefs," but in the beginning of a sentence it is, "Seamftrefs".

Throughout the Narrative, at the bottom right of each page, the printer ends with the first word from the next page.

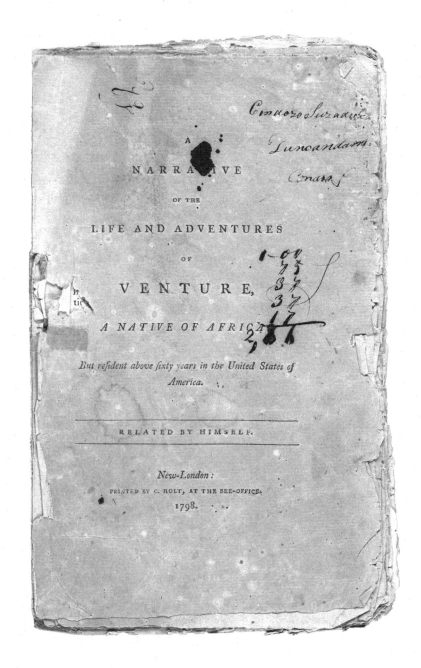

A

NARRATIVE

OF THE

LIFE AND ADVENTURES

OF

VENTURE,

A NATIVE OF AFRICA

But resident above sixty years in the United States of
America.

RELATED BY HIMSELF.

New-London:
PRINTED BY C. HOLT, AT THE BEE-OFFICE.
1798.

The Life of Venture, an African

PREFACE.

THE following account of the life of VENTURE, is a relation of simple facts, in which nothing is added in substance to what he related himself. Many other interesting and curious passages of his life might have been inserted; but on account of the bulk to which they must necessarily have swelled this narrative, they were omitted. If any should suspect the truth of what is here related, they are referred to people now living who are acquainted with most of the facts mentioned in the narrative.

The reader is here presented with an account, not of a renowned politician or warrior, but of an untutored African slave, brought into this Christian country at eight years of age, wholly destitute of all education but what he received in common with other domesticated animals, enjoying no advantages that could lead him to suppose himself superior to the beasts, his fellow servants. And if he shall derive no other advantage from perusing this narrative, he may experience those sensations of shame and indignation, that will prove him to be not wholly destitute of every noble and generous feeling.

The subject of the following pages, had he received only a common education, might have been a man of high respectability and usefulness; and had his education been suited to his genius, he might have been an ornament and an honor to human nature. It may perhaps, not be unpleasing to see the efforts of a great mind wholly uncultivated, enfeebled and depressed by slavery, and struggling under every disadvantage.——

A 2   The

The reader may here see a Franklin and a Washington, in a state of nature, or rather in a state of slavery. Destitute as he is of all education, and broken by hardships and infirmities of age, he still exhibits striking traces of native ingenuity and good sense.

This narrative exhibits a pattern of honesty, prudence and industry, to people of his own colour; and perhaps some white people would not find themselves degraded by imitating such an example.

The following account is published in compliance with the earnest desire of the subject of it, and likewise a number of respectable persons who are acquainted with him.

A nar-

A narrative of the life, &c.

❖◄◄◄❖❖❖►►►❖

CHAPTER I.

Containing an account of his life, from his birth to the time of his leaving his native country.

I WAS born at Dukandarra, in Guinea, about the year 1729. My father's name was Saungm Furro, Prince of the Tribe of Dukandarra. My father had three wives. Polygamy was not uncommon in that country, especially among the rich, as every man was allowed to keep as many wives as he could maintain. By his first wife he had three children. The eldest of them was myself, named by my father, Broteer. The other two were named Cundazo and Soozaduka. My father had two children by his second wife, and one by his third. I descended from a very large, tall and stout race of beings, much larger than the generality of people in other parts of the globe, being commonly considerable above six feet in height, and every way well proportioned.

The first thing worthy of notice which I remember was, a contention between my father and mother, on account of my father's marrying his third wife without the consent of his first and eldest, which was contrary to the custom generally observed among my countrymen. In consequence of this rupture, my mother left her husband and country, and travelled away with her three children to the eastward. I was then five years old. She took not the least sustenance along with her, to support either herself or children. I was able to
travel

travel along by her fide ; the other two of her offspring
fhe carried one on her back, and the other being a fuck-
ing child, in her arms. When we became hungry, my
mother ufed to fet us down on the ground, and gather
fome of the fruits which grew fpontaneoufly in that
climate. Thefe ferved us for food on the way. At
night we all lay down together in the moft fecure place
we could find, and repofed ourfelves until morning.
Though there were many noxious animals there ; yet
fo kind was our Almighty protector, that none of
them were ever permitted to hurt or moleft us. Thus
we went on our journey until the fecond day after our
departure from Dukandarra, when we came to the entrance of a great defert. During our travel in that we
were often affrighted with the doleful howlings and yel-
lings of wolves, lions, and other animals. After five
days travel we came to the end of this defert, and immediately entered into a beautiful and extenfive inter-
val country. Here my mother was pleafed to ftop and
feek a refuge for me. She left me at the houfe of a
very rich farmer. I was then, as I fhould judge, not
lefs than one hundred and forty miles from my native
place, feparated from all my relations and acquaintance.
At this place my mother took her farewel of me, and
fet out for her own country. My new guardian, as I
fhall call the man with whom I was left, put me into the
bufinefs of tending fheep, immediately after I was left
with him. The flock which I kept with the affiftance
of a boy, confifted of about forty. We drove them
every morning between two and three miles to pafture,
into the wide and delightful plains. When night drew
on, we drove them home and fecured them in the cote.
In this round I continued during my ftay there. One
incident which befel me when I was driving my flock
from pafture, was fo dreadful to me in that age, and is
to this time fo frefh in my memory, that I cannot help
noticing it in this place. Two large dogs fallied out of
                                        a certain

a certain house and set upon me. One of them took me by the arm, and the other by the thigh, and before their master could come and relieve me, they lacerated my flesh to such a degree, that the scars are very visible to the present day. My master was immediately sent for. He came and carried me home, as I was unable to go myself on account of my wounds. Nothing remarkable happened afterwards until my father sent for me to return home.

Before I dismiss this country, I must just inform my reader what I remember concerning this place. A large river runs through this country in a westerly course. The land for a great way on each side is flat and level, hedged in by a considerable rise of the country at a great distance from it. It scarce ever rains there, yet the land is fertile ; great dews fall in the night which refresh the soil. About the latter end of June or first of July, the river begins to rise, and gradually increases until it has inundated the country for a great distance, to the height of seven or eight feet. This brings on a slime which enriches the land surprisingly. When the river has subsided, the natives begin to sow and plant, and the vegetation is exceeding rapid. Near this rich river my guardian's land lay. He possessed, I cannot exactly tell how much, yet this I am certain of respecting it, that he owned an immense tract. He possessed likewise a great many cattle and goats. During my stay with him I was kindly used, and with as much tenderness, for what I saw, as his only son, although I was an entire stranger to him, remote from friends and relations. The principal occupations of the inhabitants there, were the cultivation of the soil and the care of their flocks. They were a people pretty similar in every respect to that of mine, except in their persons, which were not so tall and stout. They appeared to be very kind and friendly. I will now return to my departure from that place.

My

My father sent a man and horse after me. After settling with my guardian for keeping me, he took me away and went for home. It was then about one year since my mother brought me here. Nothing remarkable occured to us on our journey until we arrived safe home.

I found then that the difference between my parents had been made up previous to their sending for me. On my return, I was received both by my father and mother with great joy and affection, and was once more restored to my paternal dwelling in peace and happiness. I was then about six years old.

Not more than six weeks had passed after my return, before a message was brought by an inhabitant of the place where I lived the preceding year to my father, that that place had been invaded by a numerous army, from a nation not far distant, furnished with musical instruments, and all kinds of arms then in use; that they were instigated by some white nation who equipped and sent them to subdue and possess the country; that his nation had made no preparation for war, having been for a long time in profound peace that they could not defend themselves against such a formidable train of invaders, and must therefore necessarily evacuate their lands to the fierce enemy, and fly to the protection of some chief; and that if he would permit them they should come under his rule and protection when they had to retreat from their own possessions. He was a kind and merciful prince, and therefore consented to these proposals.

He had scarcely returned to his nation with the message, before the whole of his people were obliged to retreat from their country, and come to my father's dominions.

He gave them every privilege and all the protection his government could afford. But they had not been there longer than four days before news came to them that

that the invaders had laid waste their country, and were coming speedily to destroy them in my father's territories. This affrighted them, and therefore they immediately pushed off to the southward, into the unknown countries there, and were never more heard of.

Two days after their retreat, the report turned out to be but too true. A detachment from the enemy came to my father and informed him, that the whole army was encamped not far out of his dominions, and would invade the territory and deprive his people of their liberties and rights, if he did not comply with the following terms. These were to pay them a large sum of money, three hundred fat cattle, and a great number of goats, sheep, asses, &c.

My father told the messenger he would comply rather than that his subjects should be deprived of their rights and privileges, which he was not then in circumstances to defend from so sudden an invasion. Upon turning out those articles, the enemy pledged their faith and honor that they would not attack him. On these he relied and therefore thought it unnecessary to be on his guard against the enemy. But their pledges of faith and honor proved no better than those of other unprincipled hostile nations; for a few days after a certain relation of the king came and informed him, that the enemy who sent terms of accommodation to him and received tribute to their satisfaction, yet meditated an attack upon his subjects by surprise, and that probably they would commence their attack in less than one day, and concluded with advising him, as he was not prepared for war, to order a speedy retreat of his family and subjects. He complied with this advice.

The same night which was fixed upon to retreat, my father and his family set off about break of day. The king and his two younger wives went in one company, and my mother and her children in another. We left our dwellings in succession, and my father's company

B   went

went on first. We directed our course for a large
shrub plain, some distance off, where we intended to
conceal ourselves from the approaching enemy, until
we could refresh and rest ourselves a little. But we
presently found that our retreat was not secure. For
having struck up a little fire for the purpose of cooking
victuals, the enemy who happened to be encamped a
little distance off, had sent out a scouting party who
discovered us by the smoke of the fire, just as we were
extinguishing it, and about to eat. As soon as we had
finished eating, my father discovered the party, and
immediately began to discharge arrows at them. This
was what I first saw, and it alarmed both me and the
women, who being unable to make any resistance, immediately betook ourselves to the tall thick reeds not far
off, and left the old king to fight alone. For some
time I beheld him from the reeds defending himself with
great courage and firmness, till at last he was obliged
to surrender himself into their hands.

They then came to us in the reeds, and the very first
salute I had from them was a violent blow on the head
with the fore part of a gun, and at the same time a grasp
round the neck. I then had a rope put about my neck,
as had all the women in the thicket with me, and were
immediately led to my father, who was likewise pinioned and haltered for leading. In this condition we were
all led to the camp. The women and myself being
pretty submissive, had tolerable treatment from the enemy, while my father was closely interrogated respecting
his money which they knew he must have. But as he
gave them no account of it, he was instantly cut and
pounded on his body with great inhumanity, that he
might be induced by the torture he suffered to make
the discovery. All this availed not in the least to make
him give up his money, but he despised all the tortures
which they inflicted, until the continued exercise and
increase of torment, obliged him to sink and expire.

He

He thus died without informing his enemies of the place where his money lay. I saw him while he was thus tortured to death. The shocking scene is to this day fresh in my mind, and I have often been overcome while thinking on it. He was a man of remarkable stature. I should judge as much as six feet and six or seven inches high, two feet across his shoulders, and every way well proportioned. He was a man of remarkable strength and resolution, affable, kind and gentle, ruling with equity and moderation.

The army of the enemy was large, I should suppose consisting of about six thousand men. Their leader was called Baukurre. After destroying the old prince, they decamped and immediately marched towards the sea, lying to the west, taking with them myself and the women prisoners. In the march a scouting party was detached from the main army. To the leader of this party I was made waiter, having to carry his gun, &c.— As we were a scouting we came across a herd of fat cattle, consisting of about thirty in number. These we set upon, and immediately wrested from their keepers, and afterwards converted them into food for the army. The enemy had remarkable success in destroying the country wherever they went. For as far as they had penetrated, they laid the habitations waste and captured the people. The distance they had now brought me was about four hundred miles. All the march I had very hard tasks imposed on me, which I must perform on pain of punishment. I was obliged to carry on my head a large flat stone used for grinding our corn, weighing as I should suppose, as much as 25 pounds; besides victuals, mat and cooking utensils. Though I was pretty large and stout of my age, yet these burthens were very grievous to me, being only about six years and an half old.

We were then come to a place called Malagasco.— When we entered the place we could not see the least

appearance

appearance of either houses or inhabitants, but upon stricter search found, that instead of houses above ground they had dens in the sides of hillocks, contiguous to ponds and streams of water. In these we perceived they had all hid themselves, as I suppose they usually did upon such occasions. In order to compel them to surrender, the enemy contrived to smoke them out with faggots. These they put to the entrance of the caves and set them on fire. While they were engaged in this business, to their great surprise some of them were desperately wounded with arrows which fell from above on them. This mystery they soon found out. They perceived that the enemy discharged these arrows through holes on the top of the dens directly into the air.—Their weight brought them back, point downwards on their enemies heads, whilst they were smoking the inhabitants out. The points of their arrows were poisoned, but their enemy had an antidote for it, which they instantly applied to the wounded part. The smoke at last obliged the people to give themselves up. They came out of their caves, first spatting the palms of their hands together, and immediately after extended their arms, crossed at their wrists, ready to be bound and pinioned. I should judge that the dens above mentioned were extended about eight feet horizontally into the earth, six feet in height and as many wide. They were arched over head and lined with earth, which was of the clay kind, and made the surface of their walls firm and smooth.

The invaders then pinioned the prisoners of all ages and sexes indiscriminately, took their flocks and all their effects, and moved on their way towards the sea. On the march the prisoners were treated with clemency, on account of their being submissive and humble. Having come to the next tribe, the enemy laid siege and immediately took men, women, children, flocks, and all their valuable effects. They then went on to the next district

trict which was contiguous to the sea, called in Africa, Anamaboo. The enemies provisions were then almost spent, as well as their strength. The inhabitants knowing what conduct they had pursued, and what were their present intentions, improved the favorable opportunity, attacked them, and took enemy, prisoners, flocks and all their effects. I was then taken a second time. All of us were then put into the castle, and kept for market. On a certain time I and other prisoners were put on board a canoe, under our master, and rowed away to a vessel belonging to Rhode-Island, commanded by capt. Collingwood, and the mate Thomas Mumford. While we were going to the vessel, our master told us all to appear to the best possible advantage for sale. I was bought on board by one Robertson Mumford, steward of said vessel, for four gallons of rum, and a piece of calico, and called VENTURE, on account of his having purchased me with his own private venture. Thus I came by my name. All the slaves that were bought for that vessel's cargo, were two hundred and sixty.

CHAPTER II.

Containing an account of his life, from the time of his leaving Africa, to that of his becoming free.

AFTER all the business was ended on the coast of Africa, the ship sailed from thence to Barbadoes. After an ordinary passage, except great mortality by the small pox, which broke out on board, we arrived at the island of Barbadoes : but when we reached it, there were found out of the two hundred and sixty that sailed from Africa, not more than two hundred alive. These were all sold, except myself and three more, to the planters there.

The

The veſſel then ſailed for Rhode-Iſland, and arrived there after a comfortable paſſage. Here my maſter ſent me to live with one of his ſiſters, until he could carry me to Fiſher's Iſland, the place of his reſidence. I had then completed my eighth year. After ſtaying with his ſiſter ſome time I was taken to my maſter's place to live.

When we arrived at Narraganſet, my maſter went aſhore in order to return a part of the way by land, and gave me the charge of the keys of his trunks on board the veſſel, and charged me not to deliver them up to any body, not even to his father without his orders. To his directions I promiſed faithfully to conform. When I arrived with my maſter's articles at his houſe, my maſter's father aſked me for his ſon's keys, as he wanted to ſee what his trunks contained. I told him that my maſter intruſted me with the care of them until he ſhould return, and that I had given him my word to be faithful to the truſt, and could not therefore give him or any other perſon the keys without my maſter's directions. He inſiſted that I ſhould deliver to him the keys, threatening to puniſh me if I did not. But I let him know that he ſhould not have them let him ſay what he would. He then laid aſide trying to get them. But notwithſtanding he appeared to give up trying to obtain them from me, yet I miſtruſted that he would take ſome time when I was off my guard, either in the day time or at night to get them, therefore I ſlung them round my neck, and in the day time concealed them in my boſom, and at night I always lay with them under me, that no perſon might take them from me without being apprized of it. Thus I kept the keys from every body until my maſter came home. When he returned he aſked where VENTURE was. As I was then within hearing, I came, and ſaid, here ſir, at your ſervice. He aſked me for his keys, and I immediately took them off my neck and reached them out to him. He took them, ſtroked my hair, and commended me, ſaying in preſence of his father that

his

his young VENTURE was so faithful that he never would have been able to have taken the keys from him but by violence; that he should not fear to trust him with his whole fortune, for that he had been in his native place so habituated to keeping his word, that he would sacrifice even his life to maintain it.

The first of the time of living at my master's own place, I was pretty much employed in the house at carding wool and other houshold business. In this situation I continued for some years, after which my master put me to work out of doors. After many proofs of my faithfulness and honesty, my master began to put great confidence in me. My behavior to him had as yet been submissive and obedient. I then began to have hard tasks imposed on me. Some of these were to pound four bushels of ears of corn every night in a barrel for the poultry, or be rigorously punished. At other seasons of the year I had to card wool until a very late hour. These tasks I had to perform when I was about nine years old. Some time after I had another difficulty and oppression which was greater than any I had ever experienced since I came into this country. This was to serve two masters. James Mumford, my master's son, when his father had gone from home in the morning, and given me a stint to perform that day, would order me to do *this* and *that* business different from what my master directed me. One day in particular, the authority which my master's son had set up, had like to have produced melancholy effects. For my master having set me off my business to perform that day and then left me to perform it, his son came up to me in the course of the day, big with authority, and commanded me very arrogantly to quit my present business and go directly about what he should order me. I replied to him that my master had given me so much to perform that day, and that I must therefore faithfully complete it in that time. He then broke out into a great rage, snatched
a pitchfork

a pitchfork and went to lay me over the head therewith ; but I as soon got another and defended myself with it, or otherwise he might have murdered me in his outrage. He immediately called some people who were within hearing at work for him, and ordered them to take his hair rope and come and bind me with it. They all tried to bind me but in vain, tho' there were three assistants in number. My upstart master then desisted, put his pocket handkerchief before his eyes and went home with a design to tell his mother of the struggle with young VENTURE. He told her that their young VEN- TURE had become so stubborn that he could not con- troul him, and asked her what he should do with him. In the mean time I recovered my temper, voluntarily caused myself to be bound by the same men who tried in vain before, and carried before my young master, that he might do what he pleased with me. He took me to a gallows made for the purpose of hanging cattle on, and suspended me on it. Afterwards he ordered one of his hands to go to the peach orchard and cut him three dozen of whips to punish me with. These were brought to him, and that was all that was done with them, as I was released and went to work after hanging on the gallows about an hour.

After I had lived with my master thirteen years, be- ing then about twenty two years old, I married Meg, a slave of his who was about my age. My master owned a certain Irishman, named Heddy, who about that time formed a plan of secretly leaving his master. After he had long had this plan in meditation he suggested it to me. At first I cast a deaf ear to it, and rebuked Heddy for harboring in his mind such a rash undertaking. But after he had persuaded and much enchanted me with the prospect of gaining my freedom by such a method, I at length agreed to accompany him. Heddy next inveigled two of his fellow servants to accompany us. The place to which we designed to go was the Mississippi. Our

next

next business was to lay in a sufficient store of provisions for our voyage. We privately collected out of our master's store, six great old cheeses, two firkins of butter, and one whole batch of new bread. When we had gathered all our own clothes and some more, we took them all about midnight, and went to the water side. We stole our master's boat, embarked, and then directed our course for the Mississippi river.

We mutually confederated not to betray or desert one another on pain of death. We first steered our course for Montauk point, the east end of Long-Island. After our arrival there we landed, and Heddy and I made an incursion into the island after fresh water, while our two comrades were left at a little distance from the boat, employed at cooking. When Heddy and I had sought some time for water, he returned to our companions, and I continued on looking for my object. When Heddy had performed his business with our companions who were engaged in cooking, he went directly to the boat, stole all the clothes in it, and then travelled away for East-Hampton, as I was informed. I returned to my fellows not long after. They informed me that our clothes were stolen, but could not determine who was the thief, yet they suspected Heddy as he was missing. After reproving my two comrades for not taking care of our things which were in the boat, I advertised Heddy and sent two men in search of him. They pursued and overtook him at Southampton and returned him to the boat. I then thought it might afford some chance for my freedom, or at least a palliation for my running away, to return Heddy immediately to his master, and inform him that I was induced to go away by Heddy's address. Accordingly I set off with him and the rest of my companions for our master's, and arrived there without any difficulty. I informed my master that Heddy was the ringleader of our revolt, and that he had used us ill. He immediately put Heddy into

G   custody,

cuſtody, and myſelf and companions were well received and went to work as uſual.

Not a long time paſſed after that, before Heddy was ſent by my maſter to New-London gaol. At the cloſe of that year I was ſold to a Thomas Stanton, and had to be ſeparated from my wife and one daughter, who was about one month old. He reſided at Stonington-point. To this place I brought with me from my late maſter's, two johannes, three old Spaniſh dollars, and two thouſand of coppers, beſides five pounds of my wife's money. This money I got by cleaning gentle-men's ſhoes and drawing boots, by catching muſk-rats and minks, raiſing potatoes and carrots, &c. and by fiſhing in the night, and at odd ſpells.

All this money amounting to near twenty-one pounds York currency, my maſter's brother, Robert Stanton, hired of me, for which he gave me his note. About one year and a half after that time, my maſter purchaſ-ed my wife and her child, for ſeven hundred pounds old tenor. One time my maſter ſent me two miles af-ter a barrel of molaſſes, and ordered me to carry it on my ſhoulders. I made out to carry it all the way to my maſter's houſe. When I lived with Captain George Mumford, only to try my ſtrength, I took up on my knees a tierce of ſalt containing ſeven buſhels, and car-ried it two or three rods. Of this fact there are ſeveral eye witneſſes now living.

Towards the cloſe of the time that I reſided with this maſter, I had a falling out with my miſtreſs. This hap-pened one time when my maſter was gone to Long-Iſland a gunning. At firſt the quarrel began between my wife and her miſtreſs. I was then at work in the barn, and hearing a racket in the houſe, induced me to run there and ſee what had broken out. When I en-tered the houſe, I found my miſtreſs in a violent paſſion with my wife, for what ſhe informed me was a mere trifle ; ſuch a ſmall affair that I forbear to put my miſ-treſs

tress to the shame of having it known. I earnestly requested my wife to beg pardon of her mistress for the sake of peace, even if she had given no just occasion for offence. But whilst I was thus saying my mistress turned the blows which she was repeating on my wife to me. She took down her horse-whip, and while she was glutting her fury with it, I reached out my great black hand, raised it up and received the blows of the whip on it which were designed for my head. Then I immediately committed the whip to the devouring fire.

When my master returned from the island, his wife told him of the affair, but for the present he seemed to take no notice of it, and mentioned not a word about it to me. Some days after his return, in the morning as I was putting on a log in the fire-place, not suspecting harm from any one, I received a most violent stroke on the crown of my head with a club two feet long and as large round as a chair-post. This blow very badly wounded my head, and the scar of it remains to this day. The first blow made me have my wits about me you may suppose, for as soon as he went to renew it, I snatched the club out of his hands and dragged him out of the door. He then sent for his brother to come and assist him, but I presently left my master, took the club he wounded me with, carried it to a neighboring Justice of the Peace, and complained of my master. He finally advised me to return to my master, and live contented with him till he abused me again, and then complain. I consented to do accordingly. But before I set out for my master's, up he come and his brother Robert after me. The Justice improved this convenient opportunity to caution my master. He asked him for what he treated his slave thus hastily and unjustly, and told him what would be the consequence if he continued the same treatment towards me. After the Justice had ended his discourse with my master, he and his brother set out with me for home, one before and the other behind me.

When

When they had come to a bye place, they both dismounted their respective horses, and fell to beating me with great violence. I became enraged at this and immediately turned them both under me, laid one of them across the other, and stamped both with my feet what I would.

This occasioned my master's brother to advise him to put me off. A short time after this I was taken by a constable and two men. They carried me to a blacksmith's shop and had me hand-cuffed. When I returned home my mistress enquired much of her waiters, whether VENTURE was hand-cuffed. When she was informed that I was, she appeared to be very contented and was much transported with the news. In the midst of this content and joy, I presented myself before my mistress, shewed her my hand-cuffs, and gave her thanks for my gold rings. For this my master commanded a negro of his to fetch him a large ox chain. This my master locked on my legs with two padlocks. I continued to wear the chain peaceably for two or three days, when my master asked me with contemptuous hard names whether I had not better be freed from my chains and go to work. I answered him, No. Well then, said me, I will send you to the West-Indies or banish you, for I am resolved not to keep you. I answered him I crossed the waters to come here, and I am willing to cross them to return.

For a day or two after this not any one said much to me, until one Hempsted Miner, of Stonington, asked me if I would live with him. I answered him that I would. He then requested me to make myself discontented and to appear as unreconciled to my master as I could before that he bargained with him for me; and that in return he would give me a good chance to gain my freedom when I came to live with him. I did as he requested me. Not long after Hempsted Miner purchased me of my master for fifty-six pounds lawful. He

took

took the chain and padlocks from off me immediately after.

It may here be remembered, that I related a few pages back, that I hired out a sum of money to Mr. Robert Stanton, and took his note for it. In the fray between my master Stanton and myself, he broke open my chest containing his brother's note to me, and destroyed it. Immediately after my present master bought me, he determined to sell me at Hartford. As soon as I became apprized of it, I bethought myself that I would secure a certain sum of money which lay by me, safer than to hire it out to a Stanton. Accordingly I buried it in the earth, a little distance from Thomas Stanton's, in the road over which he passed daily. A short time after my master carried me to Hartford, and first proposed to sell me to one William Hooker of that place. Hooker asked whether I would go to the German Flats with him. I answered, No. He said I should, if not by fair means I should by foul. If you will go by no other measures, I will tie you down in my sleigh. I replied to him, that if he carried me in that manner, no person would purchase me, for it would be thought that he had a murderer for sale. After this he tried no more, and said he would not have me as a gift.

My master next offered me to Daniel Edwards, Esq. of Hartford, for sale. But not purchasing me, my master pawned me to him for ten pounds, and returned to Stonington. After some trial of my honesty, Mr. Edwards placed considerable trust and confidence in me. He put me to serve as his cup-bearer and waiter. When there was company at his house, he would send me into his cellar and other parts of his house to fetch wine and other articles occasionally for them. When I had been with him some time, he asked me why my master wished to part with such an honest negro, and why he did not keep me himself. I replied that I could not give him the reason, unless it was to convert me into cash, and

speculate

speculate with me as with other commodities. I hope that he can never justly say it was on account of my ill conduct that he did not keep me himself. Mr. Edwards told me that he should be very willing to keep me himself, and that he would never let me go from him to live, if it was not unreasonable and inconvenient for me to be parted from my wife and children; therefore he would furnish me with a horse to return to Stonington, if I had a mind for it. As Miner did not appear to redeem me I went, and called at my old master Stanton's first to see my wife, who was then owned by him. As my old master appeared much ruffled at my being there, I left my wife before I had spent any considerable time with her, and went to Colonel O. Smith's. Miner had not as yet wholly settled with Stanton for me, and had before my return from Hartford given Col. Smith a bill of sale of me. These men once met to determine which of them should hold me, and upon my expressing a desire to be owned by Col. Smith, and upon my master's settling the remainder of the money which was due to Stanton for me, it was agreed that I should live with Col. Smith. This was the third time of my being sold, and I was then thirty-one years old. As I never had an opportunity of redeeming myself whilst I was owned by Miner, though he promised to give me a chance, I was then very ambitious of obtaining it. I asked my master one time if he would consent to have me purchase my freedom. He replied that he would. I was then very happy, knowing that I was at that time able to pay part of the purchase money, by means of the money which I some time since buried. This I took out of the earth and tendered to my master, having previously engaged a free negro man to take his security for it, as I was the property of my master, and therefore could not safely take his obligation myself. What was wanting in redeeming myself, my master agreed to wait on me for, until I could

could procure it for him. I ftill continued to work for Col. Smith. There was continually fome intereft accruing on my mafter's note to my friend the free negro man above named, which I received, and with fome befides which I got by fifhing, I laid out in land adjoining my old mafter Stanton's. By cultivating this land with the greateft diligence and economy, at times when my mafter did not require my labor, in two years I laid up ten pounds. This my friend tendered my mafter for myfelf, and received his note for it.

Being encouraged by the fuccefs which I had met in redeeming myfelf, I again folicited my mafter for a further chance of completing it. The chance for which I folicited him was that of going out to work the enfuing winter. He agreed to this on condition that I would give him one quarter of my earnings. On thefe terms I worked the following winter, and earned four pounds fixteen fhillings, one quarter of which went to my mafter for the privilege, and the reft was paid him on my own account. This added to the other payments made up forty four pounds, eight fhillings, which I had paid on my own account. I was then about thirty five years old.

The next fummer I again defired he would give me a chance of going out to work. But he refufed and anfwered that he muft have my labor this fummer, as he did not have it the paft winter. I replied that I confidered it as hard that I could not have a chance to work out when the feafon became advantageous, and that I muft only be permitted to hire myfelf out in the pooreft feafon of the year. He afked me after this what I would give him for the privilege per month. I replied that I would leave it wholly with his own generofity to determine what I fhould return him a month. Well then, faid he, if fo two pounds a month. I anfwered him that if that was the leaft he would take I would be contented.

Accordingly

Accordingly I hired myself out at Fisher's Island, and earned twenty pounds; thirteen pounds six shillings of which my master drew for the privilege, and the remainder I paid him for my freedom. This made fifty-one pounds two shillings which I paid him. In October following I went and wrought six months at Long Island. In that six month's time I cut and corded four hundred cords of wood, besides threshing out seventy-five bushels of grain, and received of my wages down only twenty pounds, which left remaining a larger sum. Whilst I was out that time, I took up on my wages only one pair of shoes. At night I lay on the hearth, with one coverlet over and another under me. I returned to my master and gave him what I received of my six months labor. This left only thirteen pounds eighteen shillings to make up the full sum for my redemption. My master liberated me, saying that I might pay what was behind if I could ever make it convenient, otherwise it would be well. The amount of the money which I had paid my master towards redeeming my time, was seventy-one pounds two shillings. The reason of my master for asking such an unreasonable price, was he said, to secure himself in case I should ever come to want. Being thirty-six years old, I left Col. Smith once for all. I had already been sold three different times, made considerable money with seemingly nothing to derive it from, been cheated out of a large sum of money, lost much by misfortunes, and paid an enormous sum for my freedom.

CHAPTER

CHAPTER III.

Containing an account of his life, from the time of his purchasing his freedom to the present day.

MY wife and children were yet in bondage to Mr. Thomas Stanton. About this time I loſt a cheſt, containing beſides clothing, about thirty-eight pounds in paper money. It was burnt by accident. A ſhort time after I ſold all my poſſeſſions at Stonington, conſiſting of a pretty piece of land and one dwelling houſe thereon, and went to reſide at Long-Iſland. For the firſt four years of my reſidence there, I ſpent my time in working for various people on that and at the neighboring iſlands. In the ſpace of ſix months I cut and corded upwards of four hundred cords of wood. Many other ſingular and wonderful labors I performed in cutting wood there, which would not be inferior to thoſe juſt recited, but for brevity ſake I muſt omit them. In the aforementioned four years what wood I cut at Long-Iſland amounted to ſeveral thouſand cords, and the money which I earned thereby amounted to two hundred and ſeven pounds ten ſhillings. This money I laid up carefully by me. Perhaps ſome may enquire what maintained me all the time I was laying up money. I would inform them that I bought nothing which I did not abſolutely want. All fine clothes I deſpiſed in compariſon with my intereſt, and never kept but juſt what clothes were comfortable for common days, and perhaps I would have a garment or two which I did not have on at all times, but as for ſuperfluous finery I never thought it to be compared with a decent homeſpun dreſs, a good ſupply of money and prudence. Expenſive gatherings of my mates I commonly ſhunned, and all kinds of luxuries I was perfectly a ſtranger to ; and during the time

D   I was

I was employed in cutting the aforementioned quantity of wood, I never was at the expence of six-pence worth of spirits. Being after this labour forty years of age, I worked at various places, and in particular on Ram-Island, where I purchased Solomon and Cuff, two sons of mine, for two hundred dollars each.

It will here be remembered how much money I earned by cutting wood in four years. Besides this I had considerable money, amounting in all to near three hundred pounds. When I had purchased my two sons, I had then left more than one hundred pounds. After this I purchased a negro man, for no other reason than to oblige him, and gave for him sixty pounds. But in a short time after he run away from me, and I thereby lost all that I gave for him, except twenty pounds which he paid me previous to his absconding. The rest of my money I laid out in land, in addition to a farm which I owned before, and a dwelling house thereon. Forty four years had then completed their revolution since my entrance into this existence of servitude and misfortune. Solomon my eldest son, being then in his seventeenth year, and all my hope and dependence for help, I hired him out to one Charles Church, of Rhode-Island, for one year, on consideration of his giving him twelve pounds and an opportunity of acquiring some learning. In the course of the year, Church fitted out a vessel for a whaling voyage, and being in want of hands to man her, he induced my son to go, with the promise of giving him on his return, a pair of silver buckles, besides his wages. As soon as I heard of his going to sea, I immediately set out to go and prevent it if possible.—— But on my arrival at Church's, to my great grief, I could only see the vessel my son was in almost out of sight going to sea. My son died of the scurvy in this voyage, and Church has never yet paid me the least of his wages. In my son, besides the loss of his life, I lost equal to seventy-five pounds.

My

My other son being but a youth, still lived with me.
About this time I chartered a sloop of about thirty tons
burthen, and hired men to assist me in navigating her.
I employed her mostly in the wood trade to Rhode-
Island, and made clear of all expences above one hundred dollars with her in better than one year. I had
then become something forehanded, and being in my
forty-fourth year, I purchased my wife Meg, and thereby prevented having another child to buy, as she was
then pregnant. I gave forty pounds for her.

During my residence at Long-Island, I raised one year
with another, ten cart loads of water-melons, and lost
a great many every year besides by the thievishness of
the sailors. What I made by the water-melons I sold
there, amounted to nearly five hundred dollars. Various other methods I pursued in order to enable me to
redeem my family. In the night time I fished with set-
nets and pots for eels and lobsters, and shortly after
went a whaling voyage in the service of Col. Smith.—
After being out seven months, the vessel returned, laden
with four hundred barrels of oil. About this time, I
become possessed of another dwelling-house, and my
temporal affairs were in a pretty prosperous condition.
This and my industry was what alone saved me from being expelled that part of the island in which I resided,
as an act was passed by the select-men of the place, that
all negroes residing there should be expelled.

Next after my wife, I purchased a negro man for
four hundred dollars. But he having an inclination to
return to his old master, I therefore let him go. Shortly
after I purchased another negro man for twenty-five
pounds, whom I parted with shortly after.

Being about forty-six years old, I bought my oldest
child Hannah, of Ray Mumford, for forty-four pounds,
and she still resided with him. I had already redeemed
from slavery, myself, my wife and three children, besides three negro men.

About

About the forty-seventh year of my life, I disposed of all my property at Long-Island, and came from thence into East-Haddam. I hired myself out at first to Timothy Chapman, for five weeks, the earnings of which time I put up carefully by me. After this I wrought for Abel Bingham about six weeks. I then put my money together and purchased of said Bingham ten acres of land, lying at Haddam neck, where I now reside.—On this land I labored with great diligence for two years, and shortly after purchased six acres more of land contiguous to my other. One year from that time I purchased seventy acres more of the same man, and paid for it mostly with the produce of my other land. Soon after I bought this last lot of land, I set up a comfortable dwelling house on my farm, and built it from the produce thereof. Shortly after I had much trouble and expence with my daughter Hannah, whose name has before been mentioned in this account. She was married soon after I redeemed her, to one Isaac, a free negro, and shortly after her marriage fell sick of a mortal disease; her husband a dissolute and abandoned wretch, paid but little attention to her in her illness. I therefore thought it best to bring her to my house and nurse her there. I procured her all the aid mortals could afford, but notwithstanding this she fell a prey to her disease, after a lingering and painful endurance of it.

The physician's bills for attending her during her illness amounted to forty pounds. Having reached my fifty-fourth year, a hired two negro men, one named William Jacklin, and the other Mingo. Mingo lived with me one year, and having received his wages, run in debt to me eight dollars, for which he gave me his note. Presently after he tried to run away from me without troubling himself to pay up his note. I procured a warrant, took him, and requested him to go to Justice Throop's of his own accord, but he refusing, I took him on my shoulders, and carried him there, distant

about

about two miles. The justice asking me if I had my prisoner's note with me, and replying that I had not, he told me that I must return with him and get it. Accordingly I carried Mingo back on my shoulders, but before we arrived at my dwelling, he complained of being hurt, and asked me if this was not a hard way of treating our fellow creatures. I answered him that it would be hard thus to treat our honest fellow creatures. He then told me that if I would let him off my shoulders, he had a pair of silver shoe-buckles, one shirt and a pocket handkerchief, which he would turn out to me. I agreed, and let him return home with me on foot ; but the very following night, he slipped from me, stole my horse and has never paid me even his note. The other negro man, Jacklin, being a comb-maker by trade, he requested me to set him up, and promised to reward me well with his labor. Accordingly I bought him a set of tools for making combs, and procured him stock. He worked at my house about one year, and then run away from me with all his combs, and owed me for all his board.

Since my residence at Haddam neck, I have owned of boats, canoes and sail vessels, not less than twenty. These I mostly employed in the fishing and trafficking business, and in these occupations I have been cheated out of considerable money by people whom I traded with taking advantage of my ignorance of numbers.

About twelve years ago, I hired a whale-boat and four black men, and proceeded to Long-Island after a load of round clams. Having arrived there, I first purchased of James Webb, son of Orange Webb, six hundred and sixty clams, and afterwards, with the help of my men, finished loading my boat. The same evening, however, this Webb stole my boat, and went in her to Connecticut river, and sold her cargo for his own benefit. I thereupon pursued him, and at length, after an additional expence of nine crowns, recovered the
boat;

boat ; but for the proceeds of her cargo I never could obtain any compensation.

Four years after, I met with another loss, far superior to this in value, and I think by no less wicked means. Being going to New-London with a grand-child, I took passage in an Indian's boat, and went there with him. On our return, the Indian took on board two hogsheads of molasses, one of which belonged to Capt. Elisha Hart, of Saybrook, to be delivered on his wharf. When we arrived there, and while I was gone, at the request of the Indian, to inform Captain Hart of his arrival, and receive the freight for him, one hogshead of the molasses had been lost overboard by the people in attempting to land it on the wharf. Although I was absent at the time, and had no concern whatever in the business, as was known to a number of respectable witnesses, I was nevertheless prosecuted by this consciencious gentleman, (the Indian not being able to pay for it) and obliged to pay upwards of ten pounds lawful money, with all the costs of court. I applied to several gentlemen for counsel in this affair, and they advised me, as my adversary was rich, and threatened to carry the matter from court to court till it would cost me more than the first damages would be, to pay the sum and submit to the injury ; which I according did, and he has often since insultingly taunted me with my unmerited misfortune. Such a proceeding as this, committed on a defenceless stranger, almost worn out in the hard service of the world, without any foundation in reason or justice, whatever it may be called in a christian land, would in my native country have been branded as a crime equal to highway robbery. But Captain Hart was a *white gentleman*, and I a *poor African*, therefore it was *all right, and good enough for the black dog*.

I am now sixty nine years old. Though once strait and tall, measuring without shoes six feet one inch and

an

an half, and every way well proportioned, I am now bowed down with age and hardſhip. My ſtrength which was once equal if not ſuperior to any man whom I have ever ſeen, is now enfeebled ſo that life is a burden, and it is with fatigue that I can walk a couple of miles, ſtooping over my ſtaff. Other griefs are ſtill behind, on account of which ſome aged people, at leaſt, will pity me. My eye-ſight has gradually failed, till I am almoſt blind, and whenever I go abroad one of my grand-children muſt direct my way; beſides for many years I have been much pained and troubled with an ulcer on one of my legs. But amidſt all my griefs and pains, I have many conſolations; Meg, the wife of my youth, whom I married for love, and bought with my money, is ſtill alive. My freedom is a privilege which nothing elſe can equal. Notwithſtanding all the loſſes I have ſuffered by fire, by the injuſtice of knaves, by the cruelty and oppreſſion of falſe hearted friends, and the perfidy of my own countrymen whom I have aſſiſted and redeemed from bondage, I am now poſſeſſed of more than one hundred acres of land, and three habitable dwelling houſes. It gives me joy to think that I *have* and that I *deſerve* ſo good a character, eſpecially for *truth* and *integrity*. While I am now looking to the grave as my home, my joy for this world would be full—IF my children, Cuff for whom I paid two hundred dollars when a boy, and Solomon who was born ſoon after I purchaſed his mother—If Cuff and Solomon —O! that they had walked in the way of their father. But a father's lips are cloſed in ſilence and in grief!— Vanity of vanities, all is vanity!

F I N I S.

CERTIFICATE.

STONINGTON, *November* 3, 1798.

THESE certify, that VENTURE, a free negro man, aged about 69 years, and was, as we have ever understood, a native of Africa, and formerly a slave to Mr. James Mumford, of Fisher's-Island, in the state of New-York; who sold him to Mr. Thomas Stanton, 2d, of Stonington, in the state of Connecticut, and said Stanton sold said VENTURE to Col. Oliver Smith, of the aforesaid place. That said VENTURE hath sustained the character of a faithful servant, and that of a temperate, honest and industrious man, and being ever intent on obtaining his freedom, he was indulged by his masters after the ordinary labour on the days of his servitude, to improve the nights in fishing and other employments to his own emolument, in which time he procured so much money as to purchase his freedom from his late master Col. Smith; after which he took upon himself the name of VENTURE SMITH, and has since his freedom purchased a negro woman, called Meg, to whom he was previously married, and also his children who were slaves, and said VENTURE has since removed himself and family to the town of East-Haddam, in this state, where he hath purchased lands on which he hath built a house, and there taken up his abode.

NATHANIEL MINOR, Esq.
ELIJAH PALMER, Esq.
Capt. AMOS PALMER,
ACORS SHEFFIELD,
EDWARD SMITH.

APPENDIX CONTENTS

❖ ◄ ◄ ◄�«◼►◈◼►►›►◄ ❖

TIME LINE

❖ ◂ ◂ ◂ ◂ ◆ ◉ ◆ ▸ ▸ ▸ ❖

THE LIFE OF VENTURE SMITH

Legend:
    (dates): that are being researched, documented and refined.
    Bold dates: on which there is general agreement.
• ***Bold italic dates:*** *that are confirmed by documented records.*

    The date in the Narrative that Venture gives for his birth is "about the year 1729." The age/date on the tombstone and the title page of the Narrative, cross-referenced to the slave voyage and the runaway notice, put his birth within a range of 1727–1729. His own estimates of dates, recounted when he was about 70 years old and in failing health, are sometimes in conflict or contradict historical records.

1727-1729
    "Broteer Furro," the first son of a prince of "Dukandarra" is born.

(1737)
    Mother leaves with her three children after a dispute with her husband, returning to her own family. She leaves Venture with a prominent farmer, probably for some form of apprenticeship.

1738
    Broteer returns home, probably in the summer or fall.

• ***1738*** *October 6*
    Charming Susanna departs from Rhode Island for Africa.

(1738 fall or early 1739)
    Broteer's father is killed by a raiding army, and the boy is captured.

1739 early
Broteer is taken to Anomabu District on the Gold Coast of West Africa (now Ghana). It is unclear which slave castle he was kept in or how long he was held there.

1739 late May – early June
Broteer and other slaves are purchased by American slavers operating the Rhode Island ship Charming Susanna.

1739
Approximately early June, Charming Susanna sails from the Gold Coast.

• *1739 August 23*
Charming Susanna arrives in Bridgetown Harbor, Barbados, and sells all but four of the captives.

1739 Late August or early September
Charming Susanna sails from Barbados.

1739 September
Ship arrives in Rhode Island. Robinson Mumford temporarily places the boy with one of his sisters (probably Mercy, his oldest, who lived in Newport) to learn some English and colonial customs.

(1740)
Venture is taken from Rhode Island to the Mumford homestead on Fishers Island.

(1742 or earlier)
Robinson Mumford dies at sea and his father, Capt. George Mumford, inherits Venture.

1754
Probably in January or February, Venture marries Meg (Marget).

• *1754 March 27*
Venture runs away with two other slaves and an indentured servant and returns voluntarily sometime in April.

1754
Approximately in November, Meg gives birth to their first child, Hannah.

- *1754 end of year*
  Venture is sold to Thomas Stanton of Stonington and separated from his family.

  1756
  Meg and Hannah are sold to Thomas Stanton. Venture and Meg's first son, Solomon, is born.

  1758
  Their second son, Cuff, is born.

  (1759)
  Hempstead Miner of Stonington contracts to buy Venture from Thomas Stanton and then hires him out to Daniel Edwards of Hartford.

  (1761)
  Venture is sold for the last time to Oliver Smith Jr., who has moved to Stonington from Groton. Smith agrees to let Venture purchase himself for 85 pounds, to be paid in installments.

  (1762)
  Venture begins farming a plot of land near Thomas and Robert Stanton's Stonington farms.

  1765
  After nearly five years of making payments to Smith, largely with money earned from side jobs, Venture finally buys his freedom.

  (1767)
  Venture sells his house and land in Stonington and moves to Long Island.

  1769
  Venture purchases his two sons, Solomon and Cuff, while on Ram Island (there is disagreement as to which Ram Island).

  (1770)
  Venture buys land on Long Island.

- *1770 December 3*
  Venture buys 26 acres in Stonington.

1773
The eldest son, Solomon, dies at sea at the age of 17.

1773
Venture purchases Meg's freedom.

1774
A third son is born and named Solomon.

1774 March
Venture sells his land in Stonington.

1774 December - 1775 January
Venture leaves Long Island for Haddam, Connecticut.

1775
Venture purchases his oldest child, Hannah.

• *1775 March 3*
Venture buys 10 acres on Haddam Neck.

(1776-1777)
Venture buys six more acres on Haddam Neck.

• *1777 March 14*
Venture buys 70 additional acres from Abel Bingham and builds his home.

• *1777 August 18*
Venture and Stephen Knowlton buy 48 acres of adjoining land.

• *1778 March 8*
Venture buys Knowlton's share.

• *1781-1783*
Cuff serves in the Continental Army.

1783
Daughter Hannah dies of illness.

1798
Venture dictates his life story to Elisha Niles, and the Narrative is published by *The Bee* of New London in December.

- *1805* September *19*
  Venture Smith dies in his 77th year at Haddam Neck.

- *1809* December *17*
  Marget Smith dies in her 79th year at Haddam Neck

Meg's tombstone

The ongoing Documenting Venture Smith Project continues to
update and revise the *Time Line*. For most current version see:
beecherhouse.org link Venture Smith/Time Line

Please send comments, new information or suggestions to:
beechers@optonline.net

NARRATIVE
PUBLICATION HISTORY

❖·◄·◄·◄▭◈▭►·►·►·❖

Venture's Narrative was first published in late 1798 as a hand-stitched booklet of 32 pages (22cm by 13cm) with a plain blue cover. Starting on December 26, 1798 it was advertised for sale in *The Bee* of New London for six weeks. There is no record of how many copies were sold. From February 20 through May 14, 1799 the *Journal of the Times* in Stonington, CT advertised it for sale. Again there is no record of how many copies were sold.

In 1835, the 30th anniversary of Venture's death, the Narrative was re-published by an unidentified descendant, probably his oldest living son, Solomon. The format was similar but type size smaller. It was 24 pages (20cm by 11cm) and hand stitched with a plain blue cover. It was printed in New London, number printed unknown. Interestingly, the following final passage had been excised from the text:

> *While I am now looking to the grave as my home, my joy for this world would be full — if my children, Cuff for whom I paid two hundred dollars when a boy, and Solomon who was born soon after I purchased his mother — If Cuff and Solomon — O! that they had walked in the way of their father. But a father's lips are closed in silence and in grief! — Vanity of vanities, all is vanity!*

The Narrative was next re-published in 1897 in Middletown, Connecticut, along with information taken from oral histories of those who knew Venture or had heard relatives talk about him. The format was a 42-page (24cm by 15cm), wire-stapled booklet, number printed unknown. This re-publication occurred one year short of a century after Elisha Niles recorded the Narrative, showing continued local respect and interest in Venture.

In the late twentieth century it has been included in several printed anthologies and on-line sites. If one finds reading the original typeface difficult, several modern versions are available:

1. New London County Historical Society has published the Narrative set in modern type.
2. In *Five Black Lives*, Wesleyan University Press, 1987, (in print).
3. A transcription can be seen or downloaded from the University of North Carolina's web site:

    http://docsouth.unc.edu/neh/venture/venture.html
4. It is available in audio on a CD or can be downloaded:

    www.beecher house.org link documenting Venture Smith

E.L. Chaiter
Bates

A NARRATIVE

OF THE

LIFE & ADVENTURES

OF

VENTURE,

A NATIVE OF AFRICA;

BUT RESIDENT ABOVE SIXTY YEARS IN THE
UNITED STATES OF AMERICA.

RELATED BY HIMSELF.

NEW LONDON:—PRINTED IN 1798.

RE-PRINTED, A. D. 1835,

AND PUBLISHED BY A

DESCENDANT OF VENTURE.

Elizabeth Shaler Bates

A NARRATIVE

—OF THE—

LIFE AND ADVENTURES

—OF—

VENTURE

A NATIVE OF AFRICA,

But Resident Above Sixty Years in the United States of America.

RELATED BY HIMSELF.

New London: Printed in 1798. Reprinted A. D. 1835, and Published by a Descendant of Venture.

Revised and Republished with Traditions by H. M. SELDEN, *Haddam, Conn., 1896.*

MIDDLETOWN, CONN. :
J. S. STEWART, PRINTER AND BOOKBINDER.
1897.

The actual booklet is 1.5 times larger than this image

a. Early 18th-century map of the Gold Coast (now Ghana)

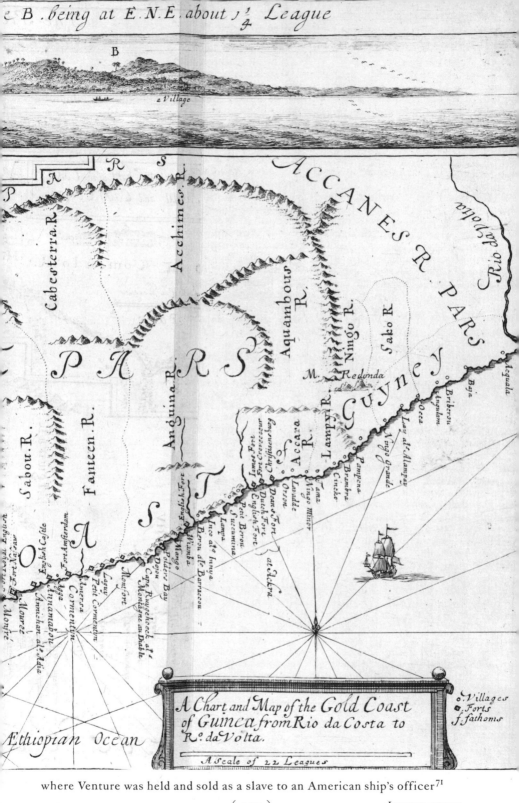

B

a Village

PARS

ACCANES R. PARS

Cabesterra R.

Acchimes R.

Rio d'Apollo

PARS

Aquambou R.

Anguina R.

PARS

Ningo R.

Sako R.

Sabou R.

Fanteen R.

M. Redunda

GUYNEY

Lampy R.

Aquala

Byia

Briberu

Ingalam

PARS

Occea

James Fort

Fort Crevecœur

Christiaenburg

Accara

Dean's Fort

Orion

English Fort

Laside

Petit Berou

Dutch Fort

Succumina

Mingo Minior

Lampa

Jama

at Acra

Pampena

Brandma

Cincko

Lato ate Alampa

Ningo Grande

Bogeu

Fort Nassau

English Castle

Fort Amsterdam

Mowre

English

Principal English

Mumfort

Adja

Annuahin ate Adja

Commentin

Petit Commentin

Lagua

Doju

Mango

Pohiery Bay

Wimba

Ineo ate Inuea

Beren d'Barracou

Cape Ruygehoeck d'r

Cape Montigne au Diable

Æthiopian Ocean

A Chart and Map of the Gold Coast of Guinea from Rio da Costa to R°. da Volta.

A Scale of 22 Leagues

o. Villages
□ Forts
f. fathoms

where Venture was held and sold as a slave to an American ship's officer[71]

ILLUSTRATIONS

The Westerly Side of the Castle at Mina

The Fort Coenr

The Fort Leidsaemheid Dutch at

The Fort Amsterdam at Cormenty

Fort Christiaansburgh at Acra at W

Fort Crevecœur at Acra at E

b. European-owned castles and forts on Guinea's Gold Coast (now Ghana)

Cabo Corso Castle and Fort Royall at E

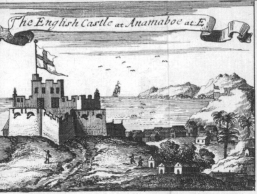

The English Castle at Anamaboe at E

The Fort Nassau Dutch at W

Fort Iames at Acra at E

The English Fort at Simpa at W

where African captives were held and sold to foreign slave ship captains[71]

ILLUSTRATIONS

NEW ENGLAND SLOOPS

❖ ◄ ◄ ◄ ◉ ◉ ◉ ► ► ► ❖

No drawing or painting is known to exist of the *Charming Susanna*, the ship that brought Venture to America in 1739. But it would have looked very much like the sloop called the *Union* (also shown on page 78).

Sloops were the workhorses of the New England-based cargo,

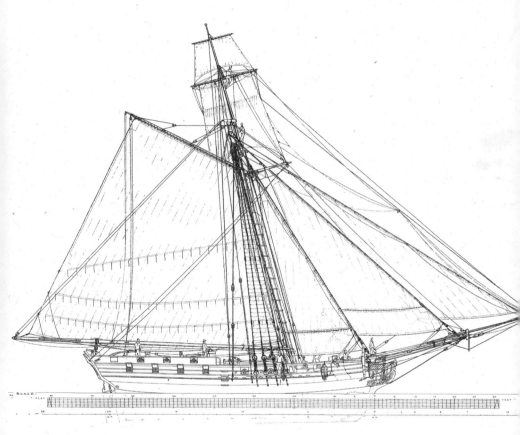

Drawings showing the 18th-century sloop *Union*, made in 1981 by Hewitt R. Jackson[72]

whaling, and slave trades in the 17th and 18th centuries. The larger ones, between 50 and 100 tons, plied the oceans, while the smaller ones worked the coasts and rivers. The *Union* was the first sloop to sail around the world. Built in Somerset, Massachusetts in 1792, it departed from Newport, Rhode Island, on August 29, 1794 and returned to Boston on July 8, 1796. It crossed the Atlantic outbound at a median speed of 80 knots a day, the equivalent of 92 miles on land.

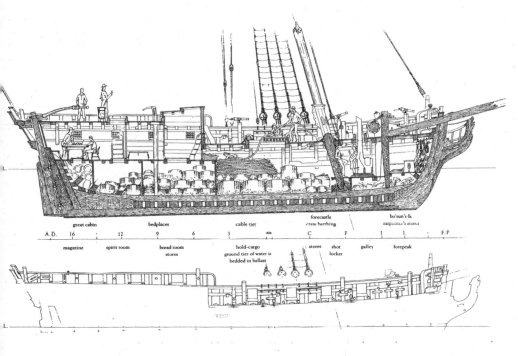

Sloops were not designed for specific tasks, but were "fitted out" for each voyage and type of cargo. When provisioning the West Indies, for example, a ship's cargo such as wood shingles, bricks and foodstuffs would be stored below in the hold, while horses, oxen, and other livestock would be secured on deck under tents. The *Charming Susanna* carried barrels of rum, tobacco, guns, and textiles to Africa and was configured to carry slaves in two main holds below decks on the return trip. One would be for men and the other for women, girls, and boys under age 15.

RUN away from George Mumford, of Fisher's-Island the 27th Instant, four Men Servants, a white Man and three Negroes, who hath taken a large two-Mast Boat, with a square Stern, and a large white Pine Canoe; the Boat's Timbers are chiefly red Cedar. The white Man named Joseph Heday, says he is a Native of Newark, in the Jerseys; a short well set Fellow, of a rudy Complection; his Cloathing when he went away was a red Whitney Great Coat, red and white flower'd Serge Jacket, a Swan-Skin strip'd ditto, lapell'd, a Pair of Leather Breeches, a Pair of Trowsers, old Shoes, &c. The Negroes are named Fortune, Venture, and Isaac; Fortune is a tall slim comely well spoken Fellow, had on a Kersey Great Coat, three Kersey Jackets, and Breeches of a dark Colour, a new Cloth colour'd Fly-Coat, with a red Lining, a blue Serge Jacket, with red Lining, a new Pair of Chocolate colour'd corded Drugget Breeches, a Pair of blue and white check'd Trowsers, two Pair of Shoes, one of them new, several Pair of Stockings, a Castor and a new Felt Hat. Venture had a Kersey dark colour'd Great Coat, three Kersey Jackets, two Pair of Breeches of the same, a new Cloth colour'd Fly-Coat, with red Shalloon Lining, a green Ratteen Jacket almost new, a trimson birded Stuff ditto, a Pair of large Oznabrigs Trowsers, a new Felt Hat, two Pair of Shoes, one Pair new, several Pair of Stockings; he is a very tall Fellow, 6 Feet 2 Inches high, thick square Shoulders, large bon'd, mark'd in the Face, or scar'd with a Knife in his own Country. Isaac is a Mustee, a short Fellow, seemingly clumsy and stiff in his Gate, bushy Head of Hair, sower Countenance, had on a Kersey Great Coat, Jacket and Breeches as aforesaid, a new Cloth colour'd Fly-Coat, with Lining, a Pair of Trowsers, of Guinea Cloth, a new Felt Hat, Shoes and Stockings as above. Stole and carried away with them, a Firkin of Butter, weighs about 60 Pound, two Cheeses weighs 64 Pounds, and Bread for the same.

Whoever takes up and secures said Run-aways, so that their Master may have them again, shall have TWENTY POUNDS, New-York Currency, Reward and all reasonable Charges paid, or equivalent for either of them; or secure the Boat, that the Owner may have her again, shall be well rewarded, by

N. GEORGE MUMFORD.

Newspaper advertisement placed by George Mumford for the capture of Venture Smith and three other escapees in 1754[73]

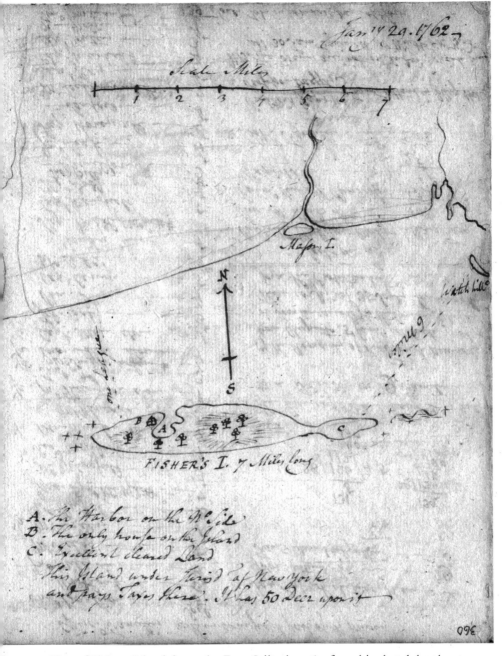

Map of Fishers Island drawn by Ezra Stiles in 1762, from his sketch book

To all People to whom these Presents shall Come, Greeting.

KNOW YE, That I Abel Bingham of East Haddam in th County of Hartford & Colony of Connecticut in new England.

For the Consideration of Twenty Pounds Lawful money

Received to my

full Satisfaction, of Venture a free negro Resident in Haddam in the County afore. Do Give, Grant, Bargain, Sell and Confirm unto the said Venture & his heirs & Assigns forever One Certain Tract of Land Lying in sd Haddam Bounded as follows (vizt) Begining at a Stake & Stones which in the Northeast Corner of Francis Chapmans Land thence westerly by sd Chapmans Land about 160 Rods to a Stake & Stones in Capt Joseph Seldins line thence Northerly Ten Rods on said Binghams Land to Bounds sett. thence Easterly about there to the fishing Cove thence by sd Cove to the first mentioned Bound Said Tract Containing Ten acres of Land. Said Venture to have liberty he & his heirs & assigns to Pass & Repass & to Cart thence sd Binghams Land in the Cart Path to the water & also liberty to Cord up his wood on the Bank, the least to sd Binghams Damage.

To Have and to Hold the above Granted and Bargained Premisses, with the Appurtenances thereof, unto him the said Venture & his Heirs and Assigns for ever, to his and their own proper Use and Behoof. AND ALSO, I the said Bingham Do for my self & my Heirs, Executors and Administrators, Covenant with the said Venture his Heirs and Assigns, That at and until the Ensealing of these Presents, I am well seized of the Premisses as a good indefeasible Estate in Fee Simple; and have good Right to Bargain and Sell the same in Manner and Form as is above Written; and that the same is free of all Incumbrances whatsoever. AND FURTHERMORE, I the said Bingham do by these Presents bind my self & my Heirs for ever, to WARRANT and defend the above granted and bargained Premisses to him the said Venture his Heirs and Assigns, against all Claims and Demands whatsoever. IN WITNESS WHEREOF I have hereunto set my Hand and Seal the 3d Day of March In the 16th Year of the Reign of Our Sovereign Lord GEORGE the Third, of GREAT-BRITAIN, &c. KING. Anno Domini, 1775 Abel Bingham & a Seal

Signed, sealed and delivered in Presence of
Samuel Huntington
Dorothy Huntington

Recorded April 18. 1775

Hartford County ss. East Haddam March 3. 1775 Personally Appeared Abel Bingham Signer & Sealer of the foregoing Instrument & Acknowledged the same to be his free act & Deed before me
Samuel Huntington Justice Peace

Copy of deed for the first Haddam Neck land purchased by Venture, "a free negro Resident in Haddam," from Abel Bingham in 1775

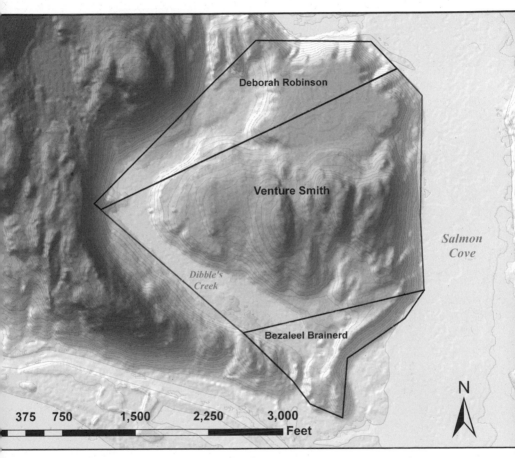

Topographical aerial view of Venture's farm at Haddam Neck, Connecticut, with overlay of 1778 boundaries by Cameron Blevins

Bill of sale from Winthrop Saltonstall for goods bought at auction on July 15, 1772, in New London, Connecticut

ENDNOTES

❖‑‑◄‑‑◄‑◄◈❖◈◗‑►‑►‑❖

Foreword (pp. ix–xiii)

1. Lyman H. Butterfield, ed., Abigail Adams to John Adams, September 22, 1774, *Adams Family Correspondence* (Harvard University Press, 1963), I, 162, pp. 12–14.

2. Donald J. Green, ed., "Taxation No Tyranny," *The Works of Samuel Johnson* (1775); (Yale University Press, 1977), 10:454.

3. Sidney Kaplan, *The Black Presence in the Era of the American Revolution, 1770-1800* (New York Graphic Society, 1973), pp. 11–13.

4. Ira Berlin, *Generations of Captivity: A History of African American Slavery* (Harvard University Press, 2003), p. 272.

Introduction (pp. 1–8)

5. Elisha Niles was a schoolteacher from the Colchester and Middle Haddam, Connecticut area, who served with the Continental Army during the Revolutionary War. Some confusion has arisen among Connecticut historians about his identity, because records show that at least five men with the name Elisha Niles lived in the region during Venture's lifetime. One branch of the family, in Groton, was known to have owned slaves, but there is no indication the man who recorded Venture's narrative owned any.

6. Venture Smith, *Preface to Narrative of the Life and Adventures of Venture, a Native of Africa, But resident above sixty years in the United States of America. Related by Himself* (The Bee, New London, Connecticut, 1798)

7. *The Interesting Narrative of the Life of Olaudah Equiano, or Gustavus Vassa, the African*, published in 1789.

8. *The Diaries of Elisha Niles (1764–1845)*, with 1969 notes by Cornelia Gross, Connecticut Historical Society.

9. Vincent Carretta, University of Maryland, *Venture Smith, One of a Kind* (paper for the Beecher House Society, 2006).

The Early Years (pp. 9–40)

10. *Voyage du Chevalier des Marchais en Guineisles voisines, et a Cayenne* (Paris, 1730).

11. Paul E. Lovejoy, *The African Background of Venture Smith* (2007).

Professor of African Studies at the University of York in Toronto, Canada, Lovejoy has done the most authoritative recent research on Venture's origins, dates, and places, which he presented in a paper prepared for a conference, in 2006, at the University of Connecticut.

12. Anomabu was the coastal district in West Africa, in present-day Ghana, known for its role as an embarkation point for slaves being taken to the West Indies and New England. The area was dotted with colonial fortresses and castles that later became holding areas for slaves. Because they were built by a variety of colonial powers — the Dutch, French, Danes, and English — there were many spellings of the name in Venture's time, including Annamabou, Anamabou, Anamaboe, Anomabu, Anemabo, and Anamabu. The authors use the accepted English spelling in Ghana — Anomabu.

13. Timothy A. Rooks, *The Social and Political Contexts Which Led to the Building of Harwood House* (Grossbritannien-Zentrum, Berlin, 2005), pp. 41; Conrad Gill, *Merchants and Mariners of the 18th Century* (London, 1961), pp. 90–95. The "factory ship" *Argyle*, anchored off the Anomabu coast in the 1730s, was skippered by Captain George Hamilton and owned by a London syndicate led by Henry Lascelle, whose family made its fortune in Barbados land and sugar, and in the American slave and provisioning trades.

14. Main sources: David Eltis, Stephen Berendt, David Richardson, and Herbert Klein, *The Atlantic Slave Trade: A Database on CD Rom* (Cambridge University Press, MA, 1999); and Jay Coughtry, *The Notorious Triangle: Rhode Island and the African Slave Trade, 1700–1807* (Temple University Press, 1981).

15. Ira Berlin, *Many Thousands Gone — The First Two Centuries of Slavery in North America* (Harvard University Press, 1998), pp. 93–95.

16. Eltis, Berendt, Richardson, and Klein, *The Atlantic Slave Trade: A Database on CD Rom.*

17. A single-masted sloop, with a fore-and-aft rig, was the workhorse of the American slave and whaling trades. The ships, averaging 40 to 60 tons unloaded, were retrofitted for whatever job was required. Oddly, very few paintings or drawings of 18th-century American sloops can be found in New England historical archives.

18. Eltis, Berendt, Richardson, and Klein, *The Atlantic Slave Trade: A Database on CD Rom.*

19. Gary B. Nash, *Forging Freedom: The Formation of Philadelphia's Black Community 1720–1840* (Harvard University Press, 1988); and Jean R. Soderlund, *Black Importation and Migration to Southeastern Pennsylvania, 1681–1810.* Proceedings of the American Philosophical Society, vol. 138; no. 2, Symposium on the Demographic Society History of the Philadelphia

Region, 1600–1860, June 1989.

20. Eltis, Berendt, Richardson, and Klein, *The Atlantic Slave Trade: A Database on CD Rom*.

21. Barry Unsworth, *Sacred Hunger* (Doubleday, 1992).

22. *The Interesting Narrative of the Life of Olaudah Equiano, or Gustavus Vassa, the African*.

23. Berlin, *Many Thousands Gone — The First Two Centuries of Slavery in North America*, pp. 106–108.

24. Robinson died around 1742 and cousin Thomas, who was first mate aboard the *Charming Susanna* on Venture's voyage, died about 1755, both on Atlantic voyages.

25. Co 28/25 in the National Archives, London, England.

26. Eltis, Berendt, Richardson, and Klein, *The Atlantic Slave Trade: A Database on CD Rom;* Berlin, *Many Thousands Gone — The First Two Centuries of Slavery in North America*.

27. Anne Farrow, Joel Lang, and Jennifer Frank, *Complicity* (The Hartford Courant, 2005). "Mumfort" is a spelling used by the English side of the family.

28. Berlin, *Many Thousands Gone — The First Two Centuries of Slavery in North America;* and Coughtry, *The Notorious Triangle: Rhode Island and the African Slave Trade*.

29. *Slavery in America* (Grolier Electronic Publishing, 1995).

30. *The Joshua Hempstead Diary, 1711 – 1758* (1901 edition, The New London County Historical Society), p. 232.

31. Ibid., p. 451.

32. Mary E. Perkins, *Chronicles of a Connecticut Farm* (Norwich, 1900), p. 72.

33. The merchants Thomas and David Mumford of Groton, Connecticut, consigned goods to Capt. Dudley Saltenstall, who shipped them on the Sloop Lyon sailing from New London the week before 12 April 1771 to Guadeloupe, West Indies, and returned to New London in May. The list of goods shown on page 32, is Saltenstall's accounting for the Mumfords, showing what was sold, to whom and at what price. The currency is in old tenor pounds. Capt. Saltenstall charged the Mumfords a five percent commission for transporting and selling the cargo. This list shows the wide variety and quantity of goods carried on a small sloop to the Carribean. List of goods (in the order presented): 21 horses, 100 barrels of flour, 49,413 shingles, 1 tierce bread, 12 barrels flour, 2 barrels flour, 2 barrels flour, 2 hogsheads fish, 14 bushels oats, 5 barrels flour, 2 barrels flour, 26 barrels flour, 14 bushels oats & a new hogshead, 1 tierce bread, 2,000 white oak staves, 2 empty hogsheads-left last voyage, 6631 shingles, 4 empty hogsheads, 1 empty hogshead; for transport-

ing and selling the goods, Capt. Saltenstall received a commission of 1,469 pounds (see image on p. 32).

34. Berlin, *Many Thousands Gone — The First Two Centuries of Slavery in North America*, p. 8.

35. Winthrop Saltenstall, Quick Claim title, 15 July 1772, New London, Connecticut. Sale of property to Dudley Saltenstall, which includes three slaves Will, Flora, and Neptune.

36. Lerone Bennett Jr., *Before the Mayflower: A History of Black America* (Johnson, 1969).

The Crucible Years (pp. 41–62)

37. In 1668 at Winthrop's request, Governor Nichols of New York made it a "Manor" and an entailed property, and the head of the Winthrop family was recognized as "Lord of the Manor" by the Crown. The Winthrops owned it for seven generations until 1863.

38. Leslie V. Brock Center for the Study of Colonial Currency, University of Virginia.

39. Robert P. Forbes, University of Connecticut, with credit to William Freehling: "In West Africa, the Fante and Akan peoples give their children a common name that is the day of the week on which they were born. Kofi (Cuff, Cuffee) means Friday. Kwame is Saturday, etc.," conversations in 2007.

40. Mark A. Yanochik, Bradley T. Ewing, and Mark Thornton, *A New Perspective on Antebellum Slavery: Public Policy and Slave Prices* (Spring, Netherlands, 2001).

41. Alice Hanson Jones, *Wealth of a Nation to Be: The American Colonies on the Eve of the Revolution* (Columbia University Press, 1980).

42. Jill Lepore, *New York Burning, Liberty, Slavery, and Conspiracy in Eighteenth-Century Manhattan* (Random House, 2005).

43. Cameron B. Blevins, *"Owned by Negro Venture": Real Estate Transactions in the Life of Venture Smith*, research for the Documenting Venture Smith Project (2007).

44. Philip J. Schwartz, *Slave Laws in Virginia* (University of Georgia Press, 1996).

45. Jackson Turner Main, *Society and Economy in Colonial Connecticut* (Princeton University Press, 1983).

46. Farrow, Lang, and Frank, *Complicity.*

47. Richard Smith in a letter to South Kingston Monthly Meeting in 1757.

The Transitional Years (pp. 63–76)

48. Berlin, *Many Thousands Gone – The First Two Centuries of Slavery in North America*, pp. 190–192.

49. Sikes and Venture appear to have had a business transaction involving land that Venture farmed in Stonington next to Thomas Stanton's farm; see *Andrew Stanton vs. Primas Sikes* case in the New London County, County Court, June 1767 term, file #536.

50. Paul E. Lovejoy referring to "Slavery in the 19th Century Kano" (Department of History dissertation, unpublished, Ahmadu Bello University, 1975) referring to the Islamic Caliphate of Sokoto, in what is now northern Nigeria.

51. Douglas Harper, *Slavery in the North* (Lancaster, PA, 2003). www.slavenorth.com/connecticut.htm

52. Berlin, *Many Thousands Gone – The First Two Centuries of Slavery in North America*, p. 239.

53. Patrica and Edward Shillingbury, *The Disposition of Slaves on the East End of Long Island From 1680 to 1796* (Shelter Island Historical Society, 2003).

54. Richard Steckel, *The Global History of Health* (Ohio State University, 2004); and John Komlos and Francesco Cinnirella, *European Heights in the Early 18th Century* (University of Munich, 2005).

55. W. J. Rorabaugh, *The Alcoholic Republic: An American Tradition* (Oxford University Press, 1981).

56. Brock Center, University of Virginia.

57. In 1765 Paul Revere sold a pair of silver shoe buckles for over 5 pounds. For Solomon, the buckles would represent more than three months' wages.

The Final Years *(pp. 77–96)*

58. Mary E. Perkins, *Chronicles of a Connecticut Farm*. Venture seemed to be surrounded all his life by large men, like himself. The Mumfords for example, were so tall that others joked that six of them constituted "thirty-six feet of Mumfords," p. 74.

59. Vincent Carretta, University of Maryland, *Venture Smith, One of a Kind*, paper for the Beecher House Society, 2006, p. 2.

60. Venture Smith, *A Narrative of the Life and Adventures of Venture Smith, a Native of Africa, But resident above sixty years in the United States of America. Related by Himself*, Revised and Republished with Traditions by H. M. Selden (J. S. Stewart, 1897), pp. 32-36.

61. Arthur Zilversmit, *The First Emancipation: The Abolition of Slavery in the North* (University of Chicago Press, 1967), p. 80.

62. Benjamin Quarles, *The Negro in the American Revolution* (Chapel Hill

Books, 1961).

63. *The American Revolution*, Microsoft Encarta 98 Encyclopedia (Microsoft Corporation).

64. Pierce Rafferty, Director, Henry L. Ferguson Museum, Fishers Island, New York, e-mails.

65. John C. Fitzpatrick, ed., *The Writings of George Washington from the Original Manuscript Sources 1745-1799* (Government Printing Ofice 1931–1944; reprint, Greenwood Press, 1970).

66. Roger Davis and Wanda Neal-Davis, *Chronology: A Historical Review, Major Events in Black History: 1492 through 1953.*

67. John Hope Franklin, *From Slavery to Freedom: A History of Negro Americans* (Knopf, 1947).

68. Abigail Adams to John Adams, September 22, 1774, from *Adams Family Papers* (Massachusetts Historical Society).

69. Robert P. Forbes, *Biblical References in the Narrative of Venture Smith* (2007), research for the Documenting Venture Smith Project.

Epilogue (pp. 105–112)

70. State of Connecticut, Department of Environmental Protection, Barn Island Wildlife Management Area.

Appendix (pp. 147–166)

71. Awnsham and Churchill, *A collection of voyages and travels, some now first printed from original manuscripts, others now first published in English . . .* vol. 5, published by J. Walthoe, London, 1732: a. Early 18th-century map of the Gold Coast of Guinea, where Venture was held and sold as a slave to an American ship's officer; b. European-owned castles and forts on Guinea's Gold Coast (region that is now Ghana) where African captives were held and sold to foreign slave ship captains for the triangular trade. These drawings, along with *A View of Cabo Corso Castle* (page 17) and *Negro's Cannoes, carrying Slaves on Board of Ships* (page 21) were done during Venture's time in West Africa by artists who actually visited the area.

72. John Boit, *Log of the Union*, edited by Edmund Hayes and illustrated by Hewitt R. Jackson (Oregon Historical Society, 1981).

73. The ad ran in *The New-York Gazette: or The Weekly Post-Boy* on April 1, 1754 and on April 8, 1754. Runaway ads were common in this paper. Two appeared on April 1 and three on April 8 for runaways either from New Jersey or headed there. Clearly, George Mumford considered Heday to be the ringleader and assumed he was trying to go home to New Jersey.

FURTHER READING

❖·◄·◄·◄◉❖◉►·►·►·❖

BOOKS:

Bailyn, Bernard. *The Ideological Origins of the American Revolution.* Harvard University Press, 1967.

Ball, Edward. *Slaves in the Family.* Ballantine Books, 1998.

Bell, Herbert C. "The West India Trade before the American Revolution," *American Historical Review* 22, (January 1917): 272–87. Dinsmore Documentation, *Classics of American Colonial History.* www.dinsdoc.com/bell-1.htm

Berlin, Ira. *Many Thousands Gone – The First Two Centuries of Slavery in North America.* Harvard University Press, 1998.

Blumrosen, Alfred W. and Ruth G. Blumrosen. *Slave Nation: How Slavery United the Colonies and Sparked the American Revolution.* Sources Books, 2005.

Coughtry, Jay. *Notorious Triangle, Rhode Island and the African Slave Trade, 1700–1807.* Temple University Press, 1981.

Davis, David Brion. *Inhuman Bondage: The Rise and Fall of Slavery in the New World.* Oxford University Press, 2006.

Engerman, Stanley L. and Robert E. Gallman, eds. *The Cambridge Economic History of the United States.* Vol. 1, *The Colonial Era.* Cambridge University Press, 1996.

Fogel, Robert and Stanley Engerman. *Time on the Cross: The Economics of American Negro Slavery.* Reissue edition: W. W. Norton, 1995.

Frey, Sylvia R. *Water from the Rock: Black Resistance in the Revolutionary Age.* Princeton University Press, 1991.

Greven, Jr., Philip J. *Four Generations: Population, Land, and Family in Colonial Andover, Massachusetts.* Cornell University Press, 1970.

Hedges, James B. *The Browns of Providence Plantations: The Colonial Years.* Brown University Press, 1968.

Horton, James Oliver and Lois E. Horton. *In Hope of Liberty.* Oxford University Press, 1997.

Horton, James Oliver and Lois E. Horton. *Slavery and the Making of America.* Oxford University Press, 2004.

Main, Jackson Turner. *Society and Economy in Colonial Connecticut.* Princeton University Press, 1985.

McCusker, John J. and Russell R. Menard. *The Economy of British America, 1607–1789*. University of North Carolina Press, 1984.

Melish, Joanne Pope. *Disowning Slavery: Gradual Emancipation and "Race" in New England, 1780–1860*. Cornell University Press, 1998.

Nelson, Marilyn. *Freedom Business*. Front Street Books, 2008.

North, Douglas C. *Economic Growth of the United States, 1790 to 1860*. W. W. Norton Press, 1961.

Piersen, William D. *Black Yankees: The Development of an Afro-American Subculture in Eighteenth-Century New England*. University of Massachusetts Press, 1988.

Poulson, Barry W. *Economic History of the United States*. Macmillan, June 1981. Smallwood, Stephanie E. *Saltwater Slavery: A Middle Passage from Africa to American Diaspora*. Harvard University Press, 2007.

Steiner, Bernard C. *History of Slavery in Connecticut*. Johns Hopkins University Press, 1893. Dinsmore Documentation, Classics of American Colonial History, Period I: 1636–1774. www.dinsdoc.com/steiner-2-0a.htm

Stewart, James Brewer. *Holy Warriors: The Abolitionists and American Slavery*. Revised edition: Hill and Wang, 1996.

Sweet, John Wood. *Bodies Politic: Negotiating Race in the American North, 1730–1830*. Johns Hopkins University Press, 2003.

Walton, Gary M. and James F. Shepherd. *The Economic Rise of Early America*. Cambridge University Press, 1979.

WEB SITES:

Africans in America (PBS). www.pbs.org/wgbh/aia/home.html

Digital History: *Learn About Slavery*. www.digitalhistory.uh.edu/modules/slavery/index.cfm

Documenting Venture Smith. www.BeecherHouse.org

Handler, Jerome S. and Michael L. Tuite Jr. *The Atlantic Slave Trade and Slave Life in the Americas: A Visual Record*. www.hitchcock.itc.virginia.edu/Slavery/index.php

Schomburg Center for Research in Black Culture. www.schomburgcenter.org

Rhode Island's Slave History. *The Unrighteous Traffic*. www.projo.com/extra/2006/slavery

The Trans-Atlantic Slave Trade Database. www.slavevoyages.org

ACKNOWLEDGMENTS

❖·◄··◄··◄◉❖◉►··►··►·❖

This book would have simply and profoundly fallen short of its intentions had it not been for a collaboration of friends and associates, most of whom are far more knowledgeable than the authors and who are as committed as we are to finding the truth.

Among these individuals, we want to single out Robert Forbes in particular, then of Yale and now the University of Connecticut, who for years was the "voice in the wilderness," trying to get Venture Smith's story told and his farm and home saved for posterity.

In keeping us on true course, we especially would like to thank David Richardson, the Beecher House Center's partner at faraway but always accessible Wilberforce Institute at Britain's Hull University; Beecher House chairman and slave scholar James Stewart of Macalester College; Robert Hall of Northeastern University for interpreting Venture; Karl Stofko, the assiduous historian of the East Haddam Church and Cemetery; Vincent Carretta of the University of Maryland; John Sweet of the University of North Carolina; Paul Lovejoy of the Tubman Institute at York University in Toronto, Canada for his invaluable, first-hand contributions on Africa; and Cameron Blevins for his honors thesis at Pomona College on Venture's Haddam Neck real estate.

We are grateful to the University of Connecticut and its diverse family of supporters, especially Philip Austin, Anne Hiskes, Veronica Makowsky, Carl Schaefer, Linda Strausbaugh, Robert Tilton, and Connecticut's state archeologist, Nicholas Bellantoni. We would also like to thank former poet laureate of Connecticut Marilyn Nelson for her inspiration throughout the Documenting Venture Smith Project.

The Connecticut Historical Society has been extremely helpful in allowing us access to vital images and documents, including a rare copy of the original 1798 Narrative of Venture Smith. In this regard, we would like to especially thank Susan Schoelwer and Richard Malley.

Special gratitude for their support and encouragement throughout this project is due to the descendants of Venture and Meg, notably Coralynne H. Jackson, Florence P. Warmsley, and the late Mandred T. Henry and Frank W. Warmsley, Sr., who both died while the book was in progress.

Our deep thanks go to our wise (and very patient) editor at Wesleyan

University Press, Suzanna Tamminen, who shared our vision and understood the importance of telling the story of Venture's struggle for freedom.

We reserve a special place for good friend Dorothea DiCecco who spent countless hours reviewing and proofreading the text, not to mention her constant and cheerful affirmation that this was a worthwhile project.

Along roads like this, there are always friends with a useful idea or suggestion, even if it's only one among dozens proffered. For those occasional but shining gems, we would like to thank Edward Baker, F. Banister, Mike Citron, Tom Crider, Jon Fasman, FOSA, Jimmie Griffin, Sarah Griswold, Phoebe Katzin, Jon Kellogg, Kazimiera Kozlowski, Alissa Krimsky, Michael Krimsky, Christine and Philip Lodewick, Mieke Maas, Elizabeth Malloy, Ted Murphy, David Nelson, Edith Pestana, Laurie and John Richardson, Virgil Rollins, Peter Rudolph, Gerald Sawyer, Steve Solley, Joshua Suhl, Peter Tillou, Louis Timolat, Carl Westmoreland, and Mike Zizka.

Thanks go also to Chandler's friend Pete Seeger for his continued support of this and other projects aimed at telling America's Freedom Story.

Chandler particularly acknowledges his late mother, Rachel Freeman Saint, who was a stalwart partner in the inception of this book and sadly could not be here for its publication. This book is dedicated to her.

George fondly thanks his wife, Paula Gibson Krimsky, for her knowledge of history, her patience, and her good humor when all three were needed.

CREDITS

American Antiquarian Society, Worcester, MA, USA/Bridgeman Art Library: 74; Arthur Pappas: chain section divider; Beinecke Rare Book and Manuscript Library, Yale University: iii, 17, 21, 36, 112-114, 156-159, 163; Cameron Blevins; 83, 85, 164, 165; Chandler Saint: 44, 48, 57, 60, 84, 87, 88, 90, 95, 103, 107, 151; Courtesy of the Connecticut Historical Society, Harford, Connecticut: 68, 75, 82, 115-143, 155; Courtesy of the Franklin Collection, Sterling Memorial Library Yale University: 73; Courtesy of the Haddam Historical Society: 154; Courtesy of The Library Company of Philadelphia: 43, 162; Courtesy of the Massachusetts Historical Society: 89; Courtesy of Mystic Seaport, G. W. Blunt Library, Mystic, CT: 19; Courtesy of the New London County Historical Society, CT: 1, 3, 32, 81; Courtesy of the Silas Bronson Library, Waterbury, CT: 49; Courtesy of the Yale University Libraries: 2, 15, 20, 38, 78, 93, 155; Dorothea V. DiCecco: 5; The Hartford Courant: 110; James Brewer Stewart Collection: 36, 166; John J. Spaulding: 92, 108; John Wood Sweet: 10, 16; Library of Congress: 8, 27, 65, 80, 81, 89, fly leaf maps; National Archives. 98; Paul Murphy, BBC Look North: 109; Oregon Historical Society, *Log of the Union: John Boit's Remarkable Voyage...* :160-161; Yale Center for British Art Paul Mellon Collection, USA/Bridgeman Art Library: 23.

Front jacket illustrations:

Upper image: Detail from the Beecher House Center map, *Venture Smith in America 1739-1805*, derived from Thomas Jefferys' *A Map of the Most Inhabited Part of New England*, 1755 edition. Library of Congress.

Lower : Detail of engraving, J. Kip artist in Awnsham and John Churchill, *A collection of voyages and travels, some now first printed from original manuscripts, others now first published in English ...*, vol. 5, published by J. Walthoe, London, 1732. Beinecke Rare Book and Manuscript Library, Yale University.

Inside covers: Front – Beecher House Center map, *Venture Smith in America 1739-1805*, derived from Thomas Jefferys' *A Map of the Most Inhabited Part of New England*, 1755 edition; rear – *Carte D'Amérique* by Guillaume De Lisle, Paris, 1780.

Robert Falcetti: photograph of George Krimsky.

Dorothea V. DiCecco: photograph of Chandler Saint.

INDEX

❖·◄·◄·◄❖◈❖◗·►·►·❖

A Narrative of the Life and Adventures of Venture, a Native of Africa (1798), 1–2, 152
advertisement for, 3–4
Biblical references in, 92
dates in, 6–7
Niles's role in, 4, 51–52
omissions from, 2, 3, 98
republication of, 100, 152–53
truthfulness of, 6
whites' certification of, 91
Nelson, Marilyn, 63, 104
New England
agriculture of, 32, 33, 34
provisioning of West Indies, 30, 33–34, 161
slave codes of, 79
slave life in, 32–35
slave population of, 25–26
slave trade of, 19–20
wolves in, 29
New London (Connecticut), Mumford family at, 47
New York City, slave revolt in, 37
Niles, Elisha, 2, 99
career of, 167 (n. 5)
religious beliefs of, 4, 92
role in Venture's Narrative, 4, 51–52
Niles family, 167 (n. 5)

P

Peter (freed slave), 87

R

Race relations, urban, 37
Reasoning, scientific, 39
Revolution, American
Fishers Island during, 80
freed blacks in, 68, 87–88, 90
northern slavery during, 80

Venture during, 74, 80, 82, 89, 90, 98
See also Continental Army
Rhode Island
farms of, 33
manumission laws of, 59
slave population of, 25
slavers of, 18
Rum, in slave trade, 19

S

Saltenstall, Captain Dudley, 169 (n. 33)
Scarification, ritual, 44–45
Seeger, Pete, 104
Sekora, John, 4
Self-determination, right of, 39
Shaw, Nathaniel, 80–81
Shelter Island (Long Island)
freed blacks at, 69
Sikes, Primas (also Primus and Sike or Sykes), 4, 73
business ventures of, 171 (n. 49)
Slave narratives, eighteenth-century, 3, 97
whites' verification of, 4
Slave revolts
in New York City, 37
in St. Domingue, 20–21
Slavers, 22
African, 15
of Rhode Island, 18
Slavery, African, 12, 15, 16, 17, 22
murgu in, 64
Slavery, northern, 4, 6, 97
daily life in, 32–35
during Revolution, 80
role in economy, 38
slave population in, 25–26
slave trade in, 19–20
Slavery, West Indian, 33
Fishers Island in, 27
mortality in, 23

Chandler B. Saint:

Is a historian and preservationist who has devoted his recent years to documenting the life and times of Venture Smith and saving his farmstead. While a studio art major at Wesleyan University in the 1960s, he met Dr. Martin Luther King, Jr., Malcolm X, and James L. Farmer. He later served with Pete Seeger and others in the emerging New England side of the civil rights movement. Greatly influenced by these giants, civil and equal rights have been central to Saint's life. For the last 40 years he has worked at restoring and preserving Early American buildings and artifacts. He has also served as a consultant in art fraud and authenticity to the U.S. Justice Department and other law enforcement agencies in the United States and Europe.

With a Connecticut family legacy dating back more than 300 years, Saint has devoted his life to preserving sites which teach America's story. In 1997, he led the effort the to save from the wrecking ball the birthplace of Harriet Beecher Stowe and her brother Henry Ward Beecher in Litchfield, Connecticut, and to establish their homestead as the core of the Beecher House Center for the Study of Equal Rights. As president of the organization, he has initiated such projects as the reenactment of the historic Lane Debates of 1834 (the first major debates held on abolition), and the Documenting Venture Smith Project, which has attracted international attention and cooperation from scholars in Britain, Canada, Africa, and the United States.

George A. Krimsky:

Is an author and journalist who spent much of his career abroad and recently returned to community journalism in his home state of Connecticut. An unabashed believer in "the invincibility of ink on paper," he notes that the story of Venture Smith would never have come to light if a newspaper had not published the former slave's narrative more than 200 years ago.

In a 16-year career with the Associated Press, Mr. Krimsky reported from Moscow before being expelled from the Soviet Union for his coverage of the dissident movement. Assigned to the Middle East, he was nominated for a Pulitzer Prize for reporting on the Lebanese civil war. He later served as World News Editor for the international news agency. In 1985, he cofounded a non-profit organization to train and assist journalists from developing nations. The International Center for Journalists in Washington, D.C., remains today the preeminent institution working with the worldwide print media.

He has worked in more than 40 countries, including a two-year tour in Central Asia to help journalists who were raised under Communism develop an independent press system.

In addition to writing on media issues for the trade press, he is the coauthor (with John Maxwell Hamilton) of a 1995 book entitled *Hold the Press: The Inside Story on Newspapers*, aimed at explaining the American newspaper industry to a general audience. He also is the author of *Bringing the World Home: Showing Readers Their Global Connections*, a newsroom handbook commissioned by the American Society of Newspaper Editors.

Since 2005, he has been a writer and columnist for the Waterbury Republican-American newspaper, where he began his journalism career 40 years earlier.

James O. Horton, Jr.:

Is the Benjamin Banneker Professor of American Studies and History, George Washington University and Historian Emeritus, National Museum of American History, Smithsonian Institution. He received his Ph.D. in history from Brandeis University. He was a Fulbright professor at the University of Munich, Germany in 1988-89 and held the John Adams Distinguished Fulbright Chair in American History at the University of Leiden, The Netherlands in 2003 and was President of the Organization of American Historians in 2004-5. He has published ten books, including *Slavery and the Making of America* (Oxford University Press, 2004) the companion book for the WNET PBS series of the same which aired in February of 2005, coauthored with Lois E. Horton; *The Landmarks of African American History* (Oxford University Press, 2005); and *Slavery and Public History: The Tough Stuff of American Memory*, (Oxford University Press, 2006), coedited with Lois E. Horton. He was appointed by President William Clinton to the Abraham Lincoln Bicentennial Commission, and was elected to the National Academy of Arts and Sciences.

Book design and composition by Chandler B. Saint, using ITC Founder's Caslon Thirty type (designed by Justin Howes).

Printed in the United States of America by Thompson-Shore on Rolland Enviro100 Print, which contains 100% post-consumer fibre, is Environmental Choice, Processed Chlorine Free and FSC Recycled certified, and manufactured in Québec by Cascades using biogas energy.

Wesleyan Univeristy Press and Thompson-Shore are members of the Green Press Initiative.